The 9 Dimensions of the Soul

David Hey

First published by O Books, 2006
O Books is an imprint of John Hunt Publishing Ltd., The Bothy, Deershot Lodge, Park Lane,
Ropley, Hants, SO24 0BE, UK
office1@o-books.net
www.o-books.net

Distribution in:

UK and Europe
Orca Book Services
orders@orcabookservices.co.uk
Tel: 01202 665432 Fax: 01202 666219 Int. code (44)

USA and Canada
NBN
custserv@nbnbooks.com
Tel: 1 800 462 6420 Fax: 1 800 338 4550

Australia
Brumby Books
sales@brumbybooks.com
Tel: 61 3 9761 5535 Fax: 61 3 9761 7095

New Zealand
Peaceful Living
books@peaceful-living.co.nz
Tel: 64 7 57 18105 Fax: 64 7 57 18513

Singapore
STP
davidbuckland@tlp.com.sg
Tel: 65 6276 Fax: 65 6276 7119

South Africa
Alternative Books
altbook@peterhyde.co.za
Tel: 021 447 5300 Fax: 021 447 1430

Text copyright David Hey 2007

Design: Stuart Davies

ISBN-13: 978 1 84694 002 6
ISBN-10: 1 84694 002 8

A CIP catalogue record for this book is available from the British Library.

Printed in the US by Maple Vail

The 9 Dimensions of the Soul

David Hey

BOOKS

Winchester, UK
Washington, USA

ACKNOWLEDGMENTS

This book could not have been written had I not met Osho, my spiritual master, and participated in the therapy and meditations he inspired.

I want to express my gratitude to Faisal, my spiritual guide for many years and my teacher in the work with Essence.

I also want to acknowledge the crucial role of Martina Jivana Werner, my publisher in Germany, who originally proposed that I write this book and who encouraged me, gently but persistently, to finish it.

I also want to thank Maria Krenz, my editor in America, who steered the text in the right direction at several key points and whose editing improved the book immeasurably.

And I need to express my love and gratitude to Pia Chiarappa, my partner and companion, who brought me so much love, laughter and tenderness during the process of writing this book.

www.davidhey.com

CONTENTS

FOREWORD

TRYING TO GET TO HEAVEN

Early in my childhood I began to realize that I had a private agenda that did not seem to be shared by others - I wanted to know who I was. I knew I was looking for something, but I had no idea what it was or how to go about finding it. Near the house where I grew up there was an open field where I used to go in the summertime. I would lie on my back and watch the magnificent clouds roll across the blue sky, feeling I had entered another dimension so vast and so far removed from my family and friends that it felt forbidden and strange - as if it was not ok to see this other dimension of life, this incredible power of presence. It was as if I was disappearing in the movement of my own breath, disappearing in the shifting forms of the clouds, like I was rolling around with the clouds up there in the sky. I felt totally absorbed in the experience of the moment, and when I would finally come out of that experience I could feel how small and narrow my daily life really was. Who am I? And what is this life actually about? It was all a big mystery and the questions kept on following me right into adulthood.

Many years later I found myself watching the clouds in quite a different setting. I was on a hillside near a Tibetan monastery outside of Kathmandu. There was the same vastness of the blue sky, but the experience was so intense that it took all my energy just to contain it, just to stay present with each ecstatic breath. The hawks circling above the trees seemed to be moving in slow motion, in a dream. Time had slowed down and the movement of my thoughts had the same slow movement of the clouds changing form in the sky. I could watch my thoughts from a tremendous distance as they slowly moved in and out of consciousness. I felt like I was the bird of prey being carried on the warm midday breeze, I was the white cloud drifting across the blue sky - I felt like an ecstatic presence that did not belong to any time or place, to any form.

In that time of my life I thought I had answered all the questions, or at least dissolved them in a reality that was beyond questions. I knew who I was. Or rather I knew who I was not – not my body, not my mind, not my conditioning, not my beliefs, not my personality. This state reminded me of Gautama Buddha's response when someone seated around the Tathagata asked, "How do we know you are enlightened?" "The earth is my witness," replied the master, touching ground with his hand. "The world is as it is, I am the way I am - and it is right." This was a time of my life when I was meditating many hours a day and receiving guidance from Tibetan lamas. It was a time of ecstasy, bliss and wonder. Life seemed like a miracle and everything had a meaning far beyond itself. Everything was so alive, even so-called inanimate objects. My spirit and my body felt translucent, permeable, as if my body was a body of light. I felt I was becoming more sensitive to everything around me, even the strange insects that came visiting me in my hut. I felt I had entered some kind of altered dimension, just as I had in childhood, only this time I was consciously entering that dimension, and it felt like discovering the reality behind all form, it felt like entering paradise.

ARRIVING IN HELL

That paradise proved to be a fragile one. Several years later I found myself in an ugly divorce with my wife, alone and without direction in life, feeling like I had been exiled to middle of nowhere. Each day was a nightmare of self-loathing, despair and anguish. I had arrived in hell and there was no exit, except possibly suicide. And I could not reconcile my experiences of bliss, ecstasy and light, with my experiences of darkness and depression, helplessness and shame. What was the point of living in the light if there was also the dark night of the soul? How could I ever integrate or understand these two experiences that were as different as night and day? The questions burned inside of me for many years. And the answers eventually came via the Enneagram, this ancient system for understanding personality.

FIRST MEETINGS WITH THE ENNEAGRAM

I had first met the Enneagram in Iran, where many of my friends at the time were involved in the work of George Gurdjieff, the Russian mystic who originally brought the Enneagram to the West. At the urging of my friends I read Ouspensky's *In Search of the Miraculous*, which had a profound effect on me. But I found Gurdjieff's renderings of the Enneagram mysterious and incomprehensible. I knew the Enneagram was a system of nine personality types and that it had something to do with spiritual growth, but beyond that, I didn't get what it was actually about.

Many years later when I met the Enneagram again, this time in India, it was a very different animal indeed. For one thing, each personality type now represented a psychologically specific profile such as dependent, avoidant, narcissistic and so on. This struck me as a welcomed improvement on the Christian profiling that dominated the earlier Enneagram, with personality types dominated by sins or character flaws such as lust, envy, pride, gluttony and avarice - defects that to me belonged more to Dante's *Inferno* or Chaucer's *Canterbury Tales* than to the modern world. The personality also started to be viewed as having both healthy and unhealthy aspects, which at least started to soften some of the judgments I had about each personality type. And I could now clearly identify my own type, the Romantic number Four. The accuracy of the description of my own personality frankly stunned me at first. How could any system have that much detailed information about me? How could a system of personality profiling know so much about my inner life, my emotional states, my beliefs, my motives? And although I was impressed by this later version of the Enneagram, I still couldn't see any practical use for this system of personality types.

ESSENCE AND THE ENNEAGRAM

It wasn't until I began to understand the role of Essence in the Enneagram that I began to understand its true value and meaning. At the core of each of the personality types of the Enneagram there is an essential quality, an important aspect of our Being, which got diminished, distorted or disowned in the process of growing up. The Enneagram is a kind of cosmic mirror that reflects back to us, not only our personality, but all the different dimensions of our Being, our true nature. For me the Enneagram was the door to finally understanding both the shadow and the light in myself – both the agony and ecstasy. Through working with Essence and the Enneagram, I experienced the truth that at the core of every issue or difficulty we face - there is Essence. This work became an important part of the path to regaining essential qualities I had lost touch with. Moreover, Essence and the Enneagram were the keys to fully understanding both the limitations of my personality and the transpersonal experiences that are beyond personality. This understanding answered the deepest longings of my heart.

INTRODUCTION AND CORE UNDERSTANDINGS

HISTORY OF THE ENNEAGRAM

The written history of the Enneagram is fragmentary and limited. What we really know about this ancient symbol is that over many centuries it has represented a way of understanding the spiritual evolution of man. There is no doubt that it had a place in the wisdom of ancient Egypt, in Christian and Jewish mysticism, and in the spiritual work of the Sufis, the mystics of Islam. We just don't know exactly what role the Enneagram actually played historically.

The oral traditions of the Sufis probably hold the core of the spiritual wisdom of the Enneagram. And the Sufis definitely are at the center of the modern understanding of the Enneagram. Gurdjieff claimed to have gotten his understanding of the Enneagram from the Sarmong Brotherhood, Sufi dervishes who lived in the region near Bukhara, in Uzbekistan. Faisal Muqaddam and A. H. Almaas, two mystics from Kuwait who developed the understanding of the different qualities of Essence, received much of their understanding of Essence from the Sufis in western Iran.

The modern lineage of the Enneagram starts with Gurdjieff, who brought the Enneagram to the West and generated great interest in it. Oscar Ichazo, a Bolivian psychotherapist, put the types in their current order. Ichazo gave the types clear profiles and he first defined the relationship between Being and personality. Claudio Naranjo, a psychiatrist from Chile, gave the types their detailed psychological profiles. The writers who helped to popularize the Enneagram in the West, such as Don Riso and Helen Palmer, come primarily through the line of Oscar Ichazo. The modern approach to Essence was developed by those who worked with Claudio Naranjo in California. They include A.H. Almaas, Faisal Muqaddam and Sandra Maitri. My understanding of the relationship between Essence and the Enneagram is strongly influenced by Faisal and the many years of work I did with him in Italy.

WHAT IS ESSENCE?

Essence refers to the different qualities of Being, which is our true nature. Essence defines the different aspects of our true nature. These are essential qualities such as Joy, Strength and Will. These qualities have very specific meanings. Each of the nine points on the circle of the Enneagram (see Diagram A) represents not only a personality type but also an essential quality. The Enneagram could also be represented by a circle divided into nine sections like a pie with nine equal pieces (see Diagram B). Each of the numbers on the Enneagram represents a personality type and an essential quality that this personality type is preoccupied with.

Even though only one quality of Essence is the primary quality our personality is preoccupied with, we are connected to all the different qualities of Essence. The Enneagram is really about Essence and separation from Essence, Being and separation from Being. The Enneagram is a mirror that reflects back to us many dimensions of ourselves. The different qualities of Essence are specific dimensions of Being. Essence is intimately connected both

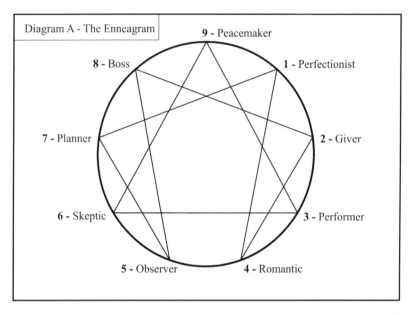

Diagram A - The Enneagram

9 - Peacemaker
8 - Boss
1 - Perfectionist
7 - Planner
2 - Giver
6 - Skeptic
3 - Performer
5 - Observer
4 - Romantic

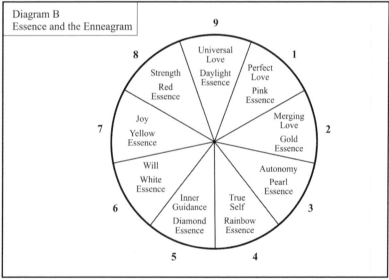

Diagram B
Essence and the Enneagram

9

8

Universal Love
Strength
Red Essence

Daylight Essence

Perfect Love
Pink Essence

1

7

Joy
Yellow Essence

Merging Love
Gold Essence

2

Will
White Essence

Autonomy
Pearl Essence

6

Inner Guidance
Diamond Essence

True Self
Rainbow Essence

3

5

4

to our Being, our true nature, and to what separates us from Being - namely our limitations, our deficiencies, what we need to heal or integrate in ourselves.

WHAT IS FIXATION?

Each of the nine personality types on the Enneagram represents a fixed attitude or a fixed stance. Hence the word "fixation" is also used to indicate the nine personality types. The fixations of the Enneagram are the fixed attitudes of each personality type. They are like different masks, different narrative styles. They are very different mental and emotional patterns, different psychological styles of protection and defense. Our fixation is a unique form of separation from Essence. Each fixation is like a deep genetic patterning that manifests in our nervous system, our body posture and our mental and emotional disposition.

When I use the word fixation I am usually talking about the whole personality, not just the primary fixation that is listed at the beginning of each chapter. To try to go against the patterns of our fixation is only to strengthen those patterns or to give them more energy. To try to get rid of our personality type or deny our fixation is a losing proposition. To fight with our ego is to fight a losing battle. The fixations stand in direct contrast to the qualities of Essence, and they tend to hide or obscure Essence in us. It is through the understanding of Essence that we can begin to rightly understand our fixation and begin to loosen the grip it has on us.

CHILDHOOD AND THE LOSS OF ESSENCE

With each stage of childhood development there is an experience of Essence. For example, Enneatype Eight, the Boss type, strongly experiences the Red Essence (Strength) in the separation phase of childhood (6-12 months of age). This is the stage where the child begins the separation process from mother and starts to explore the world beyond mother. The Eight child not only experiences the Red Essence but also experiences limitations in its freedom to explore. These limitations result in anger and a preoccupation with control issues. Boss types have a strong experience of the Strength Essence. They also feel deficient in this quality and become preoccupied with this Essence. It becomes the core of their fixation.

As we negotiate the stages of childhood, those stages are not completely integrated in us. With each stage there are things we need to learn, developmental tasks we need to complete, and things we need to give up. We experience Essence in a particular stage, and we usually experience some difficulties in integrating that stage and the corresponding essential quality. For example, Enneatype Two, the Giver, has strong experiences of the Gold Essence (Merging Love) in the symbiotic phase of childhood (0-6 months of age). This is the stage where there is a lot of sweetness between mother and child. But the Two child also develops powerful fears of separation from mother that make it difficult to integrate this stage or to let go of it. This results in the Two child being preoccupied with the loss of the Gold Essence.

Our experience in a particular phase of childhood may result in us trying to bury a certain quality of Essence because the loss of Essence was so painful. Or the child, feeling the loss of a particular Essence, may start to imitate that quality in order to compensate for this loss of self. The difficulties with each stage of childhood will affect our ability to deal successfully with subsequent stages. To the extent that developmental tasks are not completed in a particular stage, there is a corresponding loss of Essence and some regression to an earlier stage. Some qualities are more available to us than others - depending on our childhood experience in a particular stage. The greater the difficulties we experience in a particular stage of childhood, the greater the loss of Essence. Usually the stage of childhood that was especially difficult for us is where our fixation started to form.

At the moment of birth we are in full contact with Being. The light shining from the baby's eyes signals this. We are completely vulnerable and permeable. As we mature, passing through the different stages of childhood, we become more defined as an ego, but we are gradually less and less in contact with Essence or Being. The Essence in us cannot be fully supported by our environment, wounds occur and the stages of childhood cannot be fully integrated. The light shining in the child's eyes slowly gets dimmer and dimmer. With the loss of Essence, there occur energetic contractions in the physical, emotional and mental body. Something closes down. The ego tries to compensate for this loss of Essence, often by imitating a particular quality. The difficulty is that the ego cannot produce Essence. Instead it produces activity that promotes our fixation. We are transformed from a shining star into a dark star that is trying to recover the light. It feels like something was lost or something is missing in us, but we don't know what it is. Essence is what was lost and what needs to be reclaimed.

GOOD EMPTINESS AND BAD EMPTINESS

Spiritual and psychological work implies two kinds of emptiness - good emptiness and bad emptiness. Bad emptiness is the deficient emptiness of psychology and good emptiness is the transpersonal emptiness of spirituality. One is the emptiness of Gautama Buddha. Buddha's term *sunyata* indicates a transpersonal emptiness that could also be called fullness or inner spaciousness. The other emptiness is the deficient emptiness of psychology, a feeling of insufficiency, not-enough-ness or not-okay-ness. Psychological emptiness is connected to the loss of Essence in childhood. This is the deficient emptiness that the ego tries unsuccessfully to fill or hide. Deficient emptiness is not really empty but rather filled with uncomfortable physical, emotional and mental states. Ego can be viewed as resistance because inside of us there is usually some level of ego involvement in resisting our deficiencies, our feelings of not being enough or not being ok. Our discomfort is related directly to the loss of Essence, the loss of self.

Spiritual emptiness is actually the experience of Being. In that experience of Being we may feel more grounded, more alive, more relaxed, more joyful and so on – depending on which qualities of Essence we are in contact with. However, when we meet a particular quality of Essence we do not meet only the good emptiness or good feelings. For example, when we experience the Will Essence, we meet that quality in us and we may also meet the ways in which the Will Essence has been weakened or diminished in us. For example, we may feel the absence or lack of support of our father in our lives. We may also meet the ways in which we compensate for our feelings of lack of inner support. Essence opens up a radically new understanding of both these worlds of spiritual emptiness and psychological emptiness, and it also shows us precisely what the connection between these two dimensions actually is.

There is constant movement inside of us between deficient emptiness and inner spaciousness, between the experience of Essence and the experience of fixation (see Diagram C). It is basically a movement between the actual experience of Being and ego activity initiated to compensate for the lack of contact with Being. Each of the nine personality types is confused about the

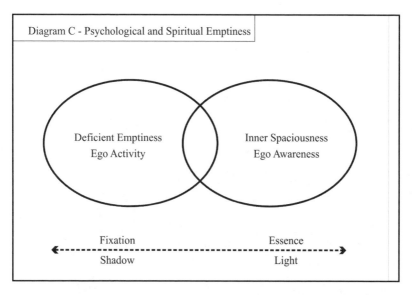

Diagram C - Psychological and Spiritual Emptiness

Deficient Emptiness
Ego Activity

Inner Spaciousness
Ego Awareness

Fixation

Essence

Shadow

Light

nature of ego activity, mistakenly believing that a certain ego activity can achieve a state of Being. Our ego, in the grip of fixation, cannot understand that its activities create separation from Being, separation from who we really are. For example, Enneatype Five, the Observer, confuses the Diamond Essence, Inner Guidance and real understanding, with intellectual activity and information gathering. This ego activity actually dulls the Diamond Essence and inhibits guidance. The Performer, Enneatype Three, confuses Autonomy with compulsive doing and self-promotion. The result is the same, namely a loss of contact with Being.

The ego is doing its best to defend against the feelings of deficient emptiness. The whole personality structure could be viewed as a "fortressing" against our limitations and deficiencies. The ego is trying to compensate for the sense of insufficiency and loss of self, but its activities generally result in more separation from Being. When ego activity is relaxed, when the effort and pushing of the ego is relinquished – there is a movement toward Essence and Being. Things happen more naturally and there is a flow to our activities.

PERSONAL AND IMPERSONAL ESSENCE

There are both personal and impersonal qualities of Essence. Some qualities, such as Universal Love (Daylight Essence) and the Absolute (Crystal Essence) tend to be more impersonal or transpersonal. These qualities tend to be more in the realm of the essential nature of existence. The issues of these qualities are more global than personal. Other qualities, such as Strength (Red Essence) and Autonomy (Pearl Essence), tend to be more personal. The personal qualities are often directly connected to differentiation and individuation, to establishing a mature personality. The personal qualities of Essence are also more intimately connected to our childhood conditioning. They are personal in every sense of the word.

Many of the qualities of Essence that I encountered in my experience of Tibetan Buddhism were of the impersonal variety. They had very little to do with individuation or psychological maturity. The more personal qualities that I encountered later in my spiritual journey, mainly through psychological work, have a lot more to do with fostering a mature personality. Developing a mature sense of self is a fundamental part of the work of recovering Essence.

EAST AND WEST

Many of our ideas about spirituality come from the East, and from India in particular. Until the last century India knew very little of anything like an individuation process, the process of becoming a unique differentiated self. Psychologically, India lived in a kind of medieval reality that involved arranged marriages that lasted for life, extended families living in a single dwelling, a caste system where everyone knew exactly where they were socially and economically. Religion and village mores dictated every aspect of life. Of course, this is no longer true for modern urban India. There was a very strong sense of "we" coupled with a very weak sense of "I". The process of becoming a distinct differentiated self was a very different process for Indians. And most Indian spiritual masters could not understand the Western process of individuation, mainly because they hadn't lived it themselves. They encouraged Westerners to drop the ego or get rid of the ego. This usually created more conflict and struggle with the ego and its activities.

The masters of the East also tended to emphasize the impersonal qualities of Essence, which are more clearly linked to the divine nature of existence or to the Absolute. At the same time they generally devalued the more personal qualities of Essence, which are linked to the individuation process. So there has been much confusion and conflict around these two realms of individuation and enlightenment, ego and Being. In India, the impersonal qualities of Essence (often devotional qualities) have also historically been given more value than the more personal qualities of Essence. For example, Brahma, Vishnu and Shiva represent divine aspects of existence. They also represent the impersonal forces of nature. Their names are chanted to help establish contact with the impersonal or transpersonal qualities they represent.

Another difficulty in the meeting of East and West is connected to alienation. In the past, the extent of the alienation from Being experienced in the West could not really be understood by the East, where the process of individuation and differentiation was less developed. The sense of identity in the East was more intimately linked to Being and Essence than it was in the West. Alienation was not a concept that was in any way familiar to the East. Tibetan lamas, for example, initially had much difficulty understanding the anxiety, depression and stress that Westerners experienced. These were states that were not generally experienced by Tibetans prior to their contact with the outside world.

At the same time, the spirituality of the East was often completely misunderstood by Westerners. Seekers from the West frequently confused fusion with spirituality. They often developed unhealthy relationships to a guru or a spiritual community, becoming dependent on them for their self worth and the meaning of their lives. This tendency for Westerners to remain in a state of fusion or codependency with a master or spiritual community inhibited their psychological maturity. The spiritual movement often became a way to avoid the individuation process, to avoid growing up.

ESSENCE AND INDIVIDUATION

Our individuation process - building a solid, stable, mature sense of self – is a requirement for any spiritual activity. Our individuation process roots us in the spiritual search and helps us contain the transpersonal experiences we encounter in meditation and other spiritual explorations. People with a weak sense of self, a weak ego structure, can often access many essential states, but they cannot contain or integrate those experiences of Being. The result can be a confused and tortured spirituality. Psychotherapy is usually the best way to build ego structure in these cases.

Without an understanding of spiritual growth and the different qualities of Essence, the individuation process can be experienced as both limited and meaningless. More importantly, an individuation process without the understanding of Essence and fixation is often flat, lacking the full maturity of an aware ego. The individuation process needs the dimension of Being, otherwise there is something missing. Conversely, the more steps we take in our individuation process, the more we can contain and integrate the different qualities of Essence.

In my early experiences of meditation, I mistakenly thought that by experiencing myself at the level of Being I was also going to take care of my individuation process - the process of becoming psychologically mature and whole. This created a conflict in me between ego and Being, between self with a small s (ego self) and Self with a capital S (essential or transpersonal self). There was a strong tendency in me at the time to get rid of the ego (as if such a thing was possible) and identify only with the more impersonal qualities of Essence. This misunderstanding created a lot of conflict and confusion in me. It also created a very immature spirituality. Wanting to live only in Essence, or only in a particular quality of Essence, creates a one-dimensional, narcissistically driven spirituality. Osho, the Indian mystic, called this "getting stuck in the beautiful places". In order to grow and mature we need to work with both the shadow and the light in us. We need to work with all the qualities of Essence and with the issues that accompany them.

THE GOAL OF THE WORK WITH ESSENCE

The goal of the work with the Essence and the Enneagram is to loosen the grip our fixation has on us and to make Essence more available to us in our daily life. This is accomplished through understanding our personality and working on ourselves with real intelligence, sincerity and perseverance. This is a process whereby we face our issues, our deficiencies, and work with them as a way of releasing Essence in us. Essence then begins to circulate more in our system and to stabilize in us. This is how the different qualities of Essence become more available to us. As we integrate the different qualities of Essence, we experience less and less involvement with our fixation and more and more contact with Being.

The work with Essence is directed toward our psychological and spiritual maturity. We develop the capacity to respond to the challenges of life with the appropriate quality of Essence, rather than with reaction and ego activity. The masks of false personality can be discarded because there is no longer anything to hide or defend. As we loosen the grip that fixation and false personality have on us, we develop an aware ego, a mature sense of self. In short, we grow up, both psychologically and spiritually. Essence and the Enneagram are powerful tools for this life-transforming work.

CHAPTER 1

CHILD'S PLAY

ENNEATYPE 1

Name: The Perfectionist (Reformer, Judge)

Essence: Perfect Love (baby love)

Color: Pink

Symbol: The Child

Passion: Anger

Fixation: Resentment

Psychology: Obsessive/compulsive

Family Deficiency: Love is a bargain, a deal

Ego Ideal: Perfection

Ego Confusion: Confuses Perfect Love (Pink Essence) with
perfectionism and activity to improve self and correct others

Mask: Always irreproachable

Specific Reaction: Self-improvement

Organ Affected: Medulla oblongata (brain stem)

THE PINK ESSENCE

The Pink Essence is about sweetness and innocence, safety and
security. It is strongly connected to the love of the baby for the
mother. It is the love for the mother's breast, for the cuddles and

schmoozing of babyhood. The Pink Essence is like pink cotton candy – it is fluffy sweet. Perfect Love gives us a kind of baby-like innocence. In Perfect Love there are no worries, no cares. When the Pink Essence is present we are literally "in the pink", meaning we are healthy and enjoying the merry-go-round of life to the fullest. We are blissfully childlike.

The Pink Essence is a state of extreme good health, both psychological and physical, both spiritual and emotional. All the neuroses and compulsions are left behind. All the judgments and the concepts are left behind. The Pink Essence relaxes and soothes both the heart and mind. It fluffs us up, it cools us down and softens us up. We become baby-like, childlike. The Pink makes us giggly. It is all the good times with mom, all her positive qualities, all the good times with grandparents and others who appreciated us in childhood. It is laughter and games - life as child's play.

When we are in contact with Perfect Love, appreciation replaces cynicism, compassion replaces judgments and criticism, playfulness replaces duty and seriousness. Taking it easy replaces pushing ourselves or improving ourselves. Perfect Love makes us young at heart. It is bubbly and light, it is refreshingly alive. It is as if we are in the presence of a bright-eyed gurgling baby, a little bliss ball of Being. This is a love that is beyond all the rules and regulations, beyond all the mundane cares of the world, beyond concepts like self-improvement or trying to get ahead. The Pink Essence could be summed up in just two words: Who cares? When we experience the Pink Essence, we just enjoy sharing. We enjoy giving and receiving, without needing to give something back or expecting recompense for our giving. We feel blissfully light. Life is a pink rose that just keeps opening. Perfect Love is pink lemonade on a beautiful summer day. The Pink Essence generates compassion and tenderness toward ourselves – loving and appreciating ourselves just the way we are. In the Pink Essence, there is an absence of seriousness, an end to being over-responsible.

THE PERFECTIONIST FIXATION

Perfectionists are generally honest, idealistic, hardworking, principled, ethical, self-disciplined, dependable and well-organized. In contact with Pink Essence, Ones are also playful, accepting, open-minded, flexible, appreciative and kind. Separated from Essence, Perfectionists tend to see only what is missing or incomplete in their surroundings. They strive to improve on how things are. In the grip of their fixation they become rigid, moralistic, tough, resentful and judgmental.

In the childhood of the Perfectionist the lack of holding or support in the family was experienced as a feeling of wrongness. There was usually an emotionally distant, over-demanding father in the childhood of Ones. They were criticized and humiliated by the judgments of others and felt they had to be without fault in order to be loved. Perfectionists are on a program of self-improvement in order to correct their sense of wrongness. The desire for perfection in the One child often meant going against their natural impulses, their desires, their spontaneity, and especially their impulses toward sex, joy and anger. They played the role of the good little boy or girl. Seriousness and rationality had a high value in the family. Joy, laughter and playfulness did not.

Ones try to get love through perfectionism, but the love they desire never really arrives. The Perfectionist personality can be understood as a disconnection from the Pink Essence, as an absence of the baby-like innocence of the Pink Essence. Enneatype One is often burdened with the tendency to correct or improve others - in a way that results in stress or conflict. Instead of generating love, Perfectionists sometimes get headaches or make themselves a headache to others. When life is seen only in terms of right or wrong the nuances tend to get lost. Tremendous energy goes into doing things right and not making mistakes – being irreproachable. And there is a feeling inside Ones that they are never good enough. Because love does not manifest through their perfectionism, Ones feel angry. And because Perfectionists feel guilty about their anger, they defend against it. The One personality can be viewed as a way to control anger. Their obsession with correctness, rightness, propriety and principle covers the anger and destructiveness that Perfectionists feel deep inside. Although Perfectionists possess a lot of personal integrity, honesty and virtue, it is angry virtue.

Enneatypes Eight, Nine and One are known as the anger types, the instinctual types or the controllers. They represent three different ways of handling anger. In the case of the Perfectionist, it is anger repressed, swallowed, invalidated. Anger is wrong (not perfect) so it cannot really be expressed in a healthy way. The unexpressed anger in Perfectionists often gives them a stiff rigid look and a judgmental mindset. Their control pattern around anger often results in smoldering resentment. Under the surface of their high-mindedness and moral rectitude there is a desire to judge and correct others that can sometimes be petty and mean-spirited. The virtue of Perfectionists is hypocritical because it prevents them from acknowledging their anger and resentment.

Perfectionists present a careful, conscientious self-image to the world. They look dependable, efficient and industrious, as well as appearing slightly over-controlled and superior (because of their high moral standards). As a package, they are tightly and carefully wrapped. There is a demanding quality in the One attitude. There is also a restrained emotional expressiveness and a denial of pleasure, which is subordinated to duty and self-discipline. The demanding aspect of the Perfectionist is the result of an inner movement that goes against others, as in the desire to inhibit the freedom or the pleasure of others. This need to control or reform others can be seen as a way for Perfectionists to distract themselves from their own unconscious desires.

MEETING THE PERFECTIONIST IN OURSELVES

When we believe we are totally right, we start to meet the Perfectionist inside ourselves. Simply stated: "I'm right and you're wrong. There's only one way - my way." We get identified with a particular point of view and it becomes like lead, heavy and inflexible. Or we get strongly identified with a certain model of existence and anything that doesn't agree with the model is condemned. Reality, however, is more complex than our beliefs, opinions or ideas about it. Sometimes it is when we are most sure of ourselves, most sure that we are right, that we are dead wrong. When we actually meet the truth, it shocks us because it is so far removed from our ideas about what is true and what is not.

Inside each of us there is often a Perfectionist waiting to come out. This is the part of us that yearns to be right, to show others the way to what is proper, irreproachable or without fault. We know we are right, that's all. Or there may be a part of us that is in strong reaction to perfectionism and prides itself on doing things wrong or breaking the rules. Or we may discover an inner critic that is secretly judging and belittling the achievements of others. There may be a part of us that feels resentful toward others who are not following the rules as we are or who are not ethical in their behavior. Our resentment usually has its roots in the Perfectionist fixation, in the ways we limit ourselves or do not go for what we really want or desire. The resentment starts to spill over onto the imperfect behaviors of others.

SHAME AND EGO DEFICIENCY

Shame is the feeling that we are flawed or defective in some way, that we are not okay the way we are. Shame is handed down from generation to generation. We are raised by wounded children in adult bodies (our parents or caretakers) who are themselves deeply shamed and deeply involved in the drama of their own childhood. Shame is collective and chronic. Our feelings of shame can be triggered by our not-okay-ness in relation to almost anything – the shape of our bodies, our gender, our social status, the size of our bank account, our needs, our sexuality, our parenting and so on. Everyone is involved in shame in some way but usually pretending they are not.

The energy of the child is often too much for the parents, and the parents have to stop that energy in some way. The child feels judged, rejected or abandoned. This gives the child the feeling of being wrong or of being too much - too sensitive, too selfish, too wild, too emotional, too loud, too strange, too something. The child starts to feel wrong in their basic life energy. In childhood, we usually experience some level of insufficient positive mirroring, the lack of feeling seen and appreciated by our parents. The child may be too different from the parents for them to mirror the child positively. Or the parental mirroring may reflect back to us only appreciation for things that are false or superficial. Normally our parents are unable to fully appreciate and adequately reflect back to us our Essence.

The newborn child is in full contact with Being. In the beginning this is primarily contact with the Essence of the soul, the True Self. The light shining from the baby's eyes reflects this contact with Being. As we move through the stages of childhood, we experience different qualities of Essence and we also experience some loss of Essence. The different stages of childhood development cannot be fully integrated and there is a corresponding loss of Essence with each stage. The ego of the child, which is being formed during these stages, starts to become preoccupied by this loss of self, this loss of Being. The more difficulty we have in a particular stage, the more there is a flattening or a diminishing of Essence. This can also result in the tendency of the ego to bury a particular quality of Essence or to fake it, pretending to experience a quality we are no longer really in touch with. The light shining from the child's eyes gets dimmer and is replaced by doubt, worry or anxiety.

The loss of self we experience in childhood results in feelings of unworthiness, lack of value. We start to feel insignificant, worthless or inadequate. One way or another, we get broken by the family system. Deep down we feel run over, betrayed. In childhood, we could not stand up to our parents. The result is shame and unworthiness. And one of the results of shame and unworthiness is that we begin to turn away from Being. And we start trying to compensate for our feelings of shame and unworthiness, our feelings of not being okay. The tragedy of childhood is that we are transformed from a shining star into a black hole. Yes, we developed an ego structure but we also lost touch with who we really are. At the same time, we cannot give up the desire to recover what was lost. There is a strong desire to get back to the light, to be the shining star we once were. At the core of all our desires – for money, power, success, love, safety, knowledge and so on - there is a desire to recover the qualities of Essence we have lost contact with.

Ego deficiency compounds our shame and unworthiness because we are never good enough, smart enough, creative enough, strong enough and so on. Our ego activity always feels deficient in some way. Our not-enough-ness never seems to go away. The reality is that our ego activity separates us from Being, from the different qualities of Essence. As a personality type or a particular ego structure, we repeat the same behaviors again and again. But the desired outcome never really arrives. We don't recover from our loss of self. We don't regain our contact with Being through the activity of the ego. In the case of Enneatype One, all the effort toward self-improvement and perfectionism doesn't produce the Pink Essence, nor does it produce the satisfaction or the recognition Ones desire. Ego activity by itself cannot produce Essence. Our ego activity is motivated by a good intention - to recover what was lost - but the mission ends in failure, with a sense of insufficiency and inadequacy. This is ego deficiency.

Essential states can be experienced through activities like mountain climbing, paragliding, meditating, making love, successfully completing a project or taking drugs – but the essential states are dependent on the activity or the substance. The ego remains in a state of chronic deficiency. When we begin to really recognize ego deficiency in ourselves, we start to feel compassion for our ego and its activities. We start to relax our ego activity.

INTEGRATING THE PINK ESSENCE

One of the challenges we meet in integrating the Pink Essence is that we meet our vulnerability. It takes tremendous strength and solidity to let go into our vulnerability. The tendency is often to defend against vulnerability because it is too dangerous or too painful, especially when it is connected to our fears, our needs or desires, our shortcomings. But we are in fact vulnerable, psychologically and physically. We live in bodies that are subject to death and disease. All our relationships ultimately end in separation. And we live on an increasingly dangerous planet. Buddha's dictum about not knowing whether tomorrow or the next life will come first is a valid way to evaluate our human condition. Becoming more aware of our vulnerability and letting go into it can be a big step toward integrating the Pink Essence and easing our hearts. We are all vulnerable and that vulnerability can be a door to our love.

A second challenge to really owning the Pink Essence is our sexual identity. Because most of us have doubts and insecurities connected to our sexual identity, we tend to judge Perfect Love as too weak, too soft, too female. The Pink challenges men to go into a softer, more receptive part of themselves. When men come in contact with the Pink Essence the penis starts to feel soft and mushy, more like a vagina than a penis – and this brings up castration anxiety. Much of the distorted male posturing we see in the world is a reaction to this castration anxiety. Perfect Love is too receptive, too female, too confronting for men's self-image. The result is often competition, challenging others or trying to prove something – all signs of this genital anxiety.

For women, there is a similar difficulty with experiencing the Pink Essence, namely the fear of surrendering to their softer, more receptive qualities. The Pink Essence, in particular, often brings up feelings of being second-rate, since the Pink Essence and female qualities in general are collectively devalued. Male qualities like Strength and Will, on the other hand, are collectively overvalued, mainly because we need them to survive in the marketplace. The result is often the same for women as it is for men, namely covering our genital anxiety with pushing, toughness and competition. And again the path toward integrating Perfect Love lies in facing some of the discomfort connected to our sexual identity and self-image.

In general, there is massive distortion in the collective consciousness around male and female qualities, often resulting in conflicts between men and women. The violence between men and women is often the result of the conflicted relationship between male and female qualities inside of us. For example, men blame women for their feelings of castration and act out violence toward women. Women blame men for their feelings of abuse and act out their feelings of anger and rage by castrating their children, especially their male children. But the real conflict is often about essential qualities and our distorted expression of them.

HEALING THE PERFECTIONIST

Our confusions about Essence often result in the creation of false qualities of Essence. When Perfectionists begin to understand that their perfectionism is not really love and not really healthy for themselves or others – then the healing can begin. They can stop improving themselves and start appreciating and enjoying life for a change. This means lightening up, relaxing the pressure to be perfect, forgiving themselves and others for their shortcomings and learning what "good enough" means.

One of the barriers to healing for the Perfectionist is their superego, the critical self. Perfectionists tend to have a very powerful inner critic. They were forced to behave like over-controlled adults at an early age - and they have internalized that control through the power of their superego. Ones need to start directing some of their anger toward this punishing critical part that can never be satisfied. They may also need to direct anger toward the demanding parental figure their superego is primarily connected to. This is the real source of their anger. Ones need to stop swallowing their anger and begin to find healthy ways to express anger. "They need to give themselves the space to express and emote and to open up some of the blocked energy inside, especially in the pelvis."

The line connecting Enneatype One and Seven indicates Essence disowned or diminished in childhood. In the case of

Perfectionists, they turned away from two Essences connected to Enneatype Seven, Joy and Mental Spaciousness. Mental Spaciousness gives us the capacity to absorb and integrate many different points of view without getting stuck in any one of them. In the childhood of the Perfectionist the critical demands of the family system gradually narrowed their vision and their capacity for maintaining a wider perspective. In contact with Mental Spaciousness, Ones are enriched by differences rather than threatened by them. Mental spaciousness also represents a kind of spacious humanism that enables us to integrate different points of view into the whole. Perfectionists need to reconnect with the wider vision and spaciousness of their original nature.

The same loss of Essence is equally true in relation to the Yellow Essence, which is Joy. In their desire to do it right, Perfectionists disconnected from the Joy Essence, from their playfulness and sense of delight. Perfectionists carry a tremendous weight on their shoulders, namely perfecting an imperfect world. It is a hard job – and sooner or later Ones need to give it up and start enjoying life. This can be a great relief. They need to reopen the door to their spontaneity and wonder, to their playfulness and innocence. The door got shut many years ago. Now the door needs to be opened. This opening to their spontaneity and desires usually needs to be a slow gentle process rather than an exuberant throwing the doors wide open. Perfectionists need to allow themselves to be silly and frivolous. They need to widen their horizons concerning what is possible and what is allowed. They need to lighten up and let go.

Another part of the healing process for Enneatype One is breaking the self-images. Perfectionists need to start letting go of their idols, their images of what is right and wrong, good and bad, weak and strong. They can retain their sense of integrity and honesty without getting stuck in the moralistic, judgmental mindset that weighs them down and kills their life energy. They need to stop caring about what other people think. Perfectionists need to focus totally on themselves and let go of what others are doing or not doing. This can be a nurturing of diversity and tolerance within themselves. This can be a reawakening of the deepest desires of their heart. When Perfectionists begin to loosen the grip of their fixation, all the qualities of Essence start to become more available.

LEADERSHIP AND ORGANIZATIONS

Ones are good decision-makers and generally make strong leaders of organizations. They have high standards and firm moral criteria from which to make decisions. They lead by teaching and by creating programs, systems and procedures. They create clear boundaries where everyone knows where they are, what they are responsible for and who reports to whom. The rules of the game are spelled out with clarity and precision. There is usually a strong directive control over people and tasks. One organizations are hierarchies with a clear chain of command. Regulations and operating procedures tend to multiply in Perfectionist organizations and there is a code of prescribed behavior that everyone adheres to. The fear of making mistakes in a One organization can result in employees who hide their mistakes or who are unwilling to voice their opinions. This may cut the One manager off from valuable feedback. Though teams tend to work well reporting to a One, the teams can lack energy and creativity.

Business gurus generally advocate a style of management that reflects their personality type. Stephen Covey, a Perfectionist business guru, advocates "principled leadership". This is a highly ethical style of management that commands respect and builds trust. One organizations thrive in stable markets and conservative business environments. They thrive on long-term planning and building a solid reputation. They are often slow to adjust to changes in market conditions. One organizations usually set high standards for quality and reliability. At their best, One organizations are both principled and functional. The rules and regulations don't strangle spontaneity and creativity, and the Perfectionist focus on details does not divorce the organization from the larger picture or from changes in market realities.

WORKING WITH ONES

Perfectionists are on time and they expect you to be on time. They expect you to be neat in your appearance and correct in your behavior. Feedback and criticism need to be given in a very conscious, diplomatic way. Directly criticizing or judging a One will harden their position and create resentment. Perfectionists need to be acknowledged for their hard work and their effort to do things right before there is any talk of things that could be done better. Never question their integrity, as they are moral beings who are trying to be a model of good behavior. Admit your mistakes and keep your promises. This will keep you on good terms with the One, whether it is the boss, a colleague or an employee. Let Ones do it their own way. They are hardworking, methodical, orderly and reliable - allow them to be that way. Never joke about morality with Ones or display inconsistent or immoral behavior. They are very sincere about their moral standards.

COLLECTIVE EXPRESSIONS OF THE PERFECTIONIST

Two countries that best represent collective expressions of Enneatype One are Switzerland and Japan. Though they represent two very different versions of the Perfectionist, the Swiss and Japanese love working together and they understand each other "perfectly". Both countries are famous for their reliability and self-discipline. There is a compulsive orderliness about both of these societies, which are over-organized to an extent not known in most countries.

In both the Japanese and the Swiss collective there is a lot of inhibition, sexual repression and frustration. There is also a rigid, narrow-minded kind of self-righteousness that puts a hard edge on the achievements of these Perfectionist cultures. A history of Calvinist Protestant morality infuses the Swiss culture with strict codes of behavior. There are many "shoulds" and many rules in these societies – and many people religiously following those rules. These are societies that live through hierarchies. In Japanese there are several ways of greeting someone, depending on their social status, and the different greetings reflect this reliance on hierarchy. In Japan, committing suicide is still a way of avoiding the shame of failure, the shame of losing face. In both cultures there is tremendous pressure to be irreproachable in one's behavior and to avoid getting caught in transgression of the moral code.

Although the United States is not a Perfectionist country (see Chapter 3) one of the legacies of America's Puritan past is that there is a lot of perfectionism in America. The thousands of self-improvement books on the shelves of bookstores across the United States are almost exclusively the work of Perfectionists. The obsession with the sex lives of film stars and politicians is also a Perfectionist trait that America shares with England, another One country. Ken Starr, the independent counsel who doggedly investigated President Clinton for years, both for his financial and sexual transgressions, is a One. Many Ones gravitated to the administration of George W. Bush, with its good-and-evil morality and its anti-terrorist rhetoric. They include John Ashcroft, the former Attorney General and Rudi Giulliani, the former mayor of New York.

The moralistic zeal of the Perfectionist often comes from the need for Ones to keep a firm grip on their own wayward desires and destructiveness. This manifests both as anger toward oneself (for not being perfect enough) and as anger toward others. Religious fundamentalists are often psychologically in the grip of the Perfectionist fixation. The ethnocentric desire to reform others - from another country, culture, religion or tribe - is part of this pattern, as with crusades, jihads and inquisitions. Besides the Pink Essence, there is a secondary Essence of the Perfectionist called Brilliancy. It is a clarity that can be likened to bright sunlight reflected on the sea or a clear mountain view on a windy day. It is real seeing - lucid perception and insight. Fundamentalists tend to mistake rigidity of opinion and extreme religious or political positions for clarity or Brilliancy. Religious orthodoxy and the literal interpretation of religious texts is part of this desire for clarity. The fundamentalists of different religions often share many of the same values and beliefs, especially their fear and hatred of liberalism and modernity.

Terrorism and fanaticism fit well into the psychology of the Perfectionist fixation - both as an expression of anger and destructiveness, and as an expression of righteousness. Regardless of the nature of the violence, or whether it is carried out through state-sponsored wars or by private groups, the psychological state of the terrorists and their sponsors is the same: "We're right and you're wrong. We insist that you share our standards." Violence becomes morally and ethically correct in this mindset. This is the place where America's conservative Christians meet the militant fundamentalists of the Islamic world, both in their many similarities and in their desire to "reform" each other.

CHAPTER 2

SWEETER THAN HONEY
ENNEATYPE TWO

Name: The Giver (Helper, Altruist)

Essence: Merging Love (precious love)

Color: Gold

Symbol: The Lovers

Passion: Pride

Fixation: Flattery

Psychology: Dependent, histrionic

Family Deficiency: Absence of love between parents

Ego Ideal: Sweetness, making others feel good

Ego Confusion: Confuses Merging Love (Gold Essence) with
    seduction, manipulation and self-inflation

Mask: Always generous, always caring

Specific Reaction: Pleasing

Organs Affected: Throat, thyroid

THE GOLD ESSENCE

The Gold Essence is about melting and merging. It is liquid
intimacy. Merging Love dissolves boundaries and melts tensions.
The post-orgasmic state of lovers is the experience of this Essence.

It is total release. It is the sweetness of a baby sleeping. In contact with the Gold Essence we are happy and content, in a state of let go, surrender and relaxation. Merging Love provides a strong sense of belonging. It lubricates the nervous system so that other qualities of Essence can flow through us. The Gold Essence brings a deep sense of contentment. It melts us. It is the sweet intimacy of fulfillment.

Strongly connected to the nervous system, the Gold Essence soothes and regenerates the nervous system. Merging Essence helps to repair and rebuild the nerves. It bathes the nervous system in healing energy. It facilitates an easy flow of energy between the nervous system, the muscles and the organs of the body. The Gold Essence restores our feelings of preciousness and value. It is warm and inviting, seductive and luxurious. It has a richness and a depth of feeling that heal us. We are truly rich when we are in contact with the Gold Essence – we don't want or need anything. It is total self-enjoyment. Merging Love restores our dignity and integrity. We are the Beloved. We are the truth of Being. In the Gold we go beyond all lies and deception. We have the courage to live our truth and claim our spirituality.

The Gold Essence is the most addictive, yummy Essence we can experience. Opiates provide an experience of the Gold Essence and its addictive power. Lovers can be experienced in the same way, as very sweet and very addictive. We crave and long for Merging Love because it brings us such powerful feelings of wellbeing, belonging, contentment. The nervous system is in constant movement between the polarities of contraction and release, and the Gold Essence is what brings release. We put ourselves through hell in order to experience this quality at the end of the marathon. Merging Essence is indeed sweeter than honey - it is our sweet reward. It is sweet warm liquid intimacy and it melts down all our resistance, all our tensions, all our desires.

THE TWO FIXATION

Givers are generally outgoing, caring and helpful. They are the nurturers of the Enneagram. Extremely sensitive to others, they easily establish rapport, making others feel at ease. They are good listeners and very empathic. They tend to bring out the best in others. In touch with Essence, Twos are generous, enthusiastic, warm and insightful. Disconnected from Essence, Twos are manipulative pleasers, taking care of others in order to get their own needs met. In the grip of their fixation, Givers become very political and very seductive, using flattery and sweetness in order to get what they want.

Enneatype Two, Three and Four comprise what are known variously as the shame types, the image types, the feeling types, the recognition types. Givers seek recognition for what they do for others. This triad of personality types can be understood as three different ways to deal with shame. Twos cover their shame through sweetness, seduction, manipulation and self-inflation. They are extremely sensitive to the needs of others and to what it takes to satisfy those needs. Their system of strategic giving can be labeled "giving to get". They satisfy other's needs in order to feel special and to get their own needs met. What they give can be described as false Gold, something very sweet and seductive, but missing the real quality of the Gold Essence. Although Givers are frequently in touch with Merging Essence, they feel deficient in this quality because it doesn't get them the attention, the recognition, the status or the power they desire. The result is that they are fixated on flattery, seduction and pleasing others – all of which produce false Gold.

As is the case with all the Enneatypes, the ego activity of the Two has a good intention, namely to produce Essence and to get the approval and love of the parents. The absence of love between the parents in the original family of Givers resulted in a corresponding lack of Gold Essence. Givers are trying to fill that deficiency, usually attempting to provide Merging Love to the opposite-sex parent. In the family system, Givers compensate for the lack of love between the parents by playing the role of daddy's little princess or mommy's little prince. They usually had a special, favored relationship with the opposite-sex parent, often catering to the needs of that parent. Satisfying that parent became their way to get what they wanted, the way to feel their value and importance.

Givers are often both the pride of the family and completely humiliated. They are both the doormats and the royalty of the family. Their core belief seems to be: "Other people's needs are more important than my own." They develop an extremely complicated relationship to their own needs. Twos get lost in the other, frequently not knowing what they really want or need. They represent the classic codependent position in their unhealthy focus on the other. At the same time, Givers can be arrogant and willful, puffed up and self-inflated. They are proud of their ability to seduce and manipulate others. Their pride, however, hides a very poor self-image and a lot of shame. And the fact that they were broken by the family system, that their will was broken, results in a compensated willfulness that often feels exaggerated or unreal to others.

Twos love flattering, pleasing, seducing and giving others what they need, especially if the others might prove useful in satisfying some of their own needs and desires. It pumps them up. And they are very good at it. Givers often make themselves indispensable in the lives of others. They do not flatter everyone, however, especially those who reject them or do not appreciate their efforts to please. When there is no return on their giving, Twos can be very aggressive. They make love or war, depending on the results of their efforts to charm and seduce the other. Twos are extremely emotional and they often appear unreliable or two-faced, mostly because the demands of pleasing others require constant shifts of attitude, opinion and stance. They are politicians. If their emotionalism and theatrics look a bit exaggerated, that's because they are.

Feeling deficient in the Gold Essence while also being obsessed with experiencing it through others, especially lovers, gives Twos a restless, unsettled quality. Givers are on the move - connecting, relating, emoting. They are very sweet, lovable and seductive - but often totally disconnected from any real sense of self. The loss of Essence robs them of their connection to themselves, to who they really are.

MEETING THE GIVER IN US

When we find ourselves in the role of the parent we naturally meet the Giver in ourselves. We face all the issues of relating through our children. When we experience the lack of healthy separation with our love ones, we also meet the Two fixation. This lack of healthy separation is variously called fusion, enmeshment, co-dependency or borrowed functioning. It means that in our intimate relating we have lost the sense of our own autonomy and value. In couple relating, we become over-connected to the other, often acting out a kind of mutual caretaking, manipulation and possessiveness that leads to low-energy relationships masquerading as love.

There are many other possible signs of meeting the Giver in us. For example, when we don't put our needs out straight but expect to get what we need by doing favors for others. Or when we get our self-value solely from others, trying to ingratiate ourselves to people we feel are more important than us. When we lose ourselves in the other, we lose our self-respect and our dignity. This often involves an inability to set limits or to say no to others, losing ourselves in taking care of other people's needs.

NEGATIVE MERGING

The Gold Essence is strongly associated with the positive merging with mother. Positive merging discharges the nervous system, as with the parasympathetic aspect of the autonomic nervous system. Negative merging is chronic tension that arises from events in the past and cannot be discharged in the same way we satisfy our hunger or our sexual desire. In the positive merging there is always some negative merging – namely feelings of frustration and discomfort. We are pushed out of our comfort zone by the negative merging with mother. The results are tension, dry heat, physical and emotional irritation, skin problems and so on. Negative merging feels something like being in the desert without water. It is an intolerable feeling, like sandpaper inside our skin. Our whole system starts to feel dry and brittle and in contraction. And our defenses are activated in order to combat these feelings of negative merging.

For the child, mother is the Gold Essence. Pregnancy puts most women into direct contact with many essential qualities. And in the first weeks of the baby's life, the mother is loaded with Essence and so is the baby. As time goes on, the mother starts to return to her normal armoring, her normal protections and defenses. The baby starts to take on more and more of the mother's negative states – such as her fear or anxiety. The Gold Essence subsides and there is more frustration and agitation in the relationship. One way to look at childhood development is as a process wherein the baby gives Essence to the mother and gradually takes on more and more of the mother's negative states.

Negative merging is inherent in the Gold Essence. The shadow of Merging Love is the agitation and the restlessness of negative merging. Negative merging is very familiar to us. It is also mom. The agitation feels familiar. We are blocked in our bodies where she is blocked. We have deficiencies where she has deficiencies. We are carrying the shadow of mom inside of us. Because we are so identified with her on the deepest levels, on a cellular level, because we spend nine months inside her body and many more months or years wrapped in her emotional states – we take this negative merging to be our own. We don't even realize how identified we are with her. Unconsciously we think mother is the Merging Essence. And we also think our lovers are the Merging Essence. In reality, mother represents both positive merging and negative merging. She is the Gold Essence and she is just a shell, just layers of negative merging. We carry inside of us the darkness of her deficiencies, her worries and her fears.

Our identification with the negative aspects of mother keeps us from separating from her on the inside. The negative merging feels like mom, it feels like home. So we keep mother near with our feelings of negative merging. For example, we may find ourselves in an extremely painful relationship that is negatively merged on many levels. We may complain about the relationship or the partner, but the relationship feels familiar to us. Letting go of the negativity means letting go of mama. If the relationship ends, we feel distraught. We are attached to the relationship, painful though it is, because it prevents us from feeling our anxieties around really separating from mother and standing on our own two feet.

Our compulsions and addictions are driven by our feelings of negative merging. We charge into our compulsions and addictions as if they are going to give us relief, but they don't, or at least not for long. And the repetition of our compulsions creates more feelings of anxiety and agitation – and more negative merging. Our compulsions make us feel weak and out of control. They trigger the judgments of our inner critic, as in superego attacks. And the whole process feels familiar - feels like mama. So despite the discomfort of negative merging, we don't want to give it up because giving it up means separation from mother.

The answer to negative merging is healthy separation from mother - on the inside. When we stop idealizing or demonizing our mother, when we start to humanize her, realizing that she is neither all good or all bad – things get better. We start to see mother as a human being, with her strong points and her weak points. We can also begin to see our intimate partner more realistically when this happens, rather than seeing them as a devil or a saint. We stop asking our partner to regulate us or discharge our tension - we stop demanding that they give us the Gold Essence. As we mature and differentiate from mother, the image we are holding of her on the inside starts to disappear. This brings up the fear of separation from mother, but it also holds out the possibility of healthy psychological separation from her. We need to separate from mother in order to have mature relationships and take our rightful place in the world.

INTEGRATING THE GOLD ESSENCE

The Gold Essence challenges us to face the issues of mother and our lack of separation from her. The pain of negative merging keeps us from daring to really go into the Merging Essence. It is too painful. In many cases, we have closed ourselves to the Gold Essence, closed ourselves to love, in order to avoid the discomfort of negative merging. So we need to begin to face the pain of negative merging, the agitation and frustration of it, in order to start enjoying the Gold again. This means exploring all the issues related to mother – such as wanting her, lack of healthy separation from her, idealizing her or devaluing her, and so on. The more we resolve the issues of mother inside of us, the more available becomes the Gold Essence and the less powerful becomes the negative merging.

Another aspect of integrating the Gold Essence is acknowledging how powerful the collective negative merging really is. This means acknowledging all the past karma of our planet, the collective suffering that our ancestors have lived through. We need to acknowledge how damaged the collective reality of our world is, how much suffering and pain is being created in every moment. By acknowledging this pain and anguish, we begin to make Merging Love more available, while at the same time diminishing our unconscious fears of the pain of negative merging. Opening our hearts to the collective pain of our planet, opening our compassion for the suffering of others, supports our contact with the Gold Essence. In Tibetan Buddhism compassion is a quality that releases the Gold, thereby making other qualities of Essence more available.

We need to learn to self-soothe in times of stress and agitation. We need to begin to find the orgasmic response inside of us, rather than expecting our intimate partner to give us this experience. This means quieting the nervous system down through meditation and other techniques. It also means physical activity that helps us to release the Gold – such as sports or yoga or other physical exercise that gives us enjoyment or pleasure. Often very simple exercises, like lying on the back with the knees bent and gently rocking the pelvis, can start to release the Gold Essence in us. We need to become less dependent on the other for our experiences of Merging Essence.

HEALING THE GIVER

The first step toward healing for Givers is facing how they got broken by the original family, how humiliated and shamed they were in childhood. The unhealthy bond they had in childhood, usually with the opposite-sex parent, was a constant source of heartache for the Two. They lost their sense of dignity, self-respect and value. They sold out for love – a love that could never be consummated or satisfied. And they need to see how much the adult ego activity of pleasing and giving and making others feel good is still hooked up to the parent they bonded with. Only by facing the pain of this parental relationship, the rage and frustration in it, can they begin to regain their sense of personal integrity.

A second step for Twos in the direction of healing is to begin to put the focus of their attention squarely on themselves. That entails focusing on their needs rather than the needs of others. It also means that they start to learn to put their needs out straight rather than manipulating others into giving them what they want. It means they also need to be able to take a "no" sometimes - that they can accept the fact that others cannot always give them what they want. Givers also need to begin the process of self-validating or self-valuing. Rather than expecting others to give them a sense of value, appreciation and recognition, Twos need to start the process of honoring their own Being, respecting their own talents and abilities, trusting their own truth and sticking by it. They need to begin to stand up for themselves in a way that gives them dignity and self-respect. They need to be their own person.

The third step for Givers to take in healing themselves is to begin the process of making the Gold Essence more available. Rather than trying to manifest Merging Love through their relationships, Givers need to find activities they can do alone to release the Gold Essence. They need to begin to realize that this quality resides inside them, that they only need to surrender to it, let go into it. Givers need to reconnect with the pleasure of the Gold Essence. Often they are in so much activity around relating that their pleasure gets derailed.

And the last step toward healing is connected to the line between Two and Four. In childhood Twos turned their backs on two essential qualities of the Romantic – the True Self and Compassion. They need to reconnect to their authentic sense of self, their soul self. They need to know that the Beloved is not out there in someone else, but in their own heart. They need to reconnect with the Green Essence, which is Compassion, real love for others and for themselves, real generosity of the heart.

LEADERSHIP AND ORGANIZATIONS

Unlike the Perfectionist organization, Two organizations are not based on following rules and regulations, but rather on bending rules to fit the needs of clients and employees alike. Two organizations are strong in customer service, in providing customers with what they really need - except when these organizations are government monopolies. Customer satisfaction has a very high priority. Two organizations are usually very good in responding to market changes, to the changing needs of their clients. They often have a charismatic nurturing leader who is caring for both clients and employees. The organization becomes a benevolent mothering enterprise, a family affair. Employee programs in Two companies are often strong in areas like human resources development, medical assistance, profit sharing and so forth. The personal human aspect of doing business tends to take precedence over cost control, strategic planning or technological innovation.

Twos don't normally exercise a traditional boss role or a managerial style of leadership. The Two style of leadership is more often humanistic. Two leaders tend to see management as a support function. They want to influence their employees in a benevolent way. Givers are very good in support roles and in bringing the big players together. And Twos are great in managing the boss. Twos readily take the initiative - they know what needs to be done and they do it. In whatever role they are playing in an organization, Twos need a lot of social contact – and they need to be in an organization that allows for this.

HOW TO WORK WITH TWOS

Relationships have a high priority for Twos. Take time to nurture your relationship with them. Fast impersonal talk will not get you much with Twos. Get to know what they feel and what they value emotionally. Compliment them. Acknowledge them for what they give and do for others. They need to feel loved and needed. Do not take them for granted. Thank them when they do something for you. Let them meet your needs and appreciate them for providing what you need. Don't try to bully them or dominate them. It won't work. Emphasize the big picture rather than getting caught up in details and specifics. Never embarrass a Two or aggressively criticize them – they will seek revenge. Instead, talk about your real needs and the Giver will meet you there.

COLLECTIVE EXPRESSIONS OF THE GIVER

Italy and Thailand are archetypal Two countries. Italy tends to be a more social expression of the Two, Thailand a more sexual expression. In both cultures there is an absence of a solid sense of self, an absence of personal boundaries and the ability to set limits. In both cultures people live in a strong fusion with family and with groups. Independent activity and individual responsibility are not hallmarks of these cultures. Relating takes precedence over results. Communication takes precedence over action. Deadlines don't mean much – relationships mean a lot.

In Italy there are more mobile phones per capita than any other country in the world. Connecting, communicating, relating – all have a very high value in Italy. Italians can literally talk all day, and if the situation permits, they will do just that. They also like to scream and shout – at each other. And the louder their voices get, the better they like it. It is as if there is a tremendous narcissistic need that gets filled by relating – any kind of relating. Often Italians don't really seem to care what they are talking about, they are just happy to be talking. Contact between people is often emotional, but when you scratch beneath the surface of this emotionality, there is often nothing there. There are usually no deep feelings beneath the dramas that look so intense. To a certain extent emotions need to be contained in order for us to generate depth of feeling. Italy represents zero emotional containment. Histrionics is the name for this behavior - drama for the sake of drama. This style of relating demands that others see you and listen to you. Relating gives one status, importance and self-worth. But the feelings don't go very deep. This is why Italians are sometimes screaming at each other one moment and hugging each other the next.

Where in other countries there is fierce competition, as in the telecommunications sector, in Italy there's often none. Instead of competition there is a monopoly that completely controls prices and services. And in order to deal with that monopoly you need to know someone who can influence that organization on your behalf. Government organizations often function like little mafias that you need to know how to deal with. In the same government agency you can get five different answers to the same question. The rules of the game are very flexible, anything is possible and it always helps to know someone who is in a position to do you a favor. Everything happens through relating. It is no wonder that Italians survive by seducing others who are worthy of seduction. Mussolini sucks up to Hitler. Berlusconi sucks up to Bush. It's a national pastime.

Italians are experts in strategic giving. Relating, pleasing and having cozy relationships with others is something like investment banking. Something comes back from your investments in relating. A little gift or some special attention can truly be strategic. If nothing comes back, you limit your relating investment in that person. If a lot comes back, you increase your investment. Italians want to be seen as generous and giving, but they are primarily doing favors for each other as a way of building up credits for future needs. The giving is often directly related to satisfying personal needs.

Food has a unique place in the Two culture. Both Italy and Thailand have very sophisticated national cuisines and both countries are obsessed by food. Food plays a central role in these cultures and in the Two fixation, both as a substitute for the Gold Essence and as a way to avoid the uncomfortable feelings of negative merging. One of the common greetings in Thailand is "Have you eaten?" And people eat many times a day in Thailand. In both cultures food serves as a substitute for love and as a major vehicle for relating, especially group relating.

CHAPTER 3

MASTER OF MYSELF
ENNEATYPE 3

Name: The Performer (Achiever, Doer)

Essence: Autonomy (maturity)

Color: Pearl

Symbol: Lord Krishna

Passion: Deceit, self-deception

Fixation: Action, role playing, generating

Psychology: Type A personality, workaholic

Family Deficiency: Absence of bonding between family members

Ego Ideal: Connectedness, emotional contact, bonding

Ego Confusion: Confuses Autonomy (Pearl Essence) with performing and self-promotion

Mask: Always competent

Specific Reaction: Compulsive doing, achieving

Organs Affected: Heart, pericardium

THE PEARL ESSENCE

The Rainbow Essence is the Essence of the soul, our essential identity. The Pearl Essence is the embodiment of the soul. It is essential Autonomy. It represents integration, actualization and maturity. The Pearl dissolves the layers of ego that are fixation and false personality. The Pearl goes beyond ego activity. In the integration of the Pearl, our activities are informed by Being. The Pearl Essence is the link between the spirit and the flesh, between action and Being, between Zorba the Greek and Gautama the Buddha. The Pearl enables us to bring our self-realization into our daily life, fulfilling our soul purpose. It is the vehicle for the actualization of Being.

The Rainbow Essence, our essential identity, is our True Self. The Rainbow Essence is the essential sense of "I", whereas the Pearl is the essential sense of "I am". The Pearl Essence is the flesh of the True Self, the embodiment of who we really are. The Pearl facilitates the manifestation of Essence in our lives. The Pearl and the Rainbow Essence are the two most significant personal qualities of Essence. They are personal in the sense that we are all different souls, different individuated selves - different beings of light. In the personal Essence of the Pearl we are totally involved, totally connected and totally present. Our actions bring integration and fulfillment. Action based on ego identification and fixation brings separation and alienation.

The Pearl Essence is the field between the Absolute and human activity, between the experience of Essence and its expression. It is the consciousness that gives us full contact with the body, with the material world - and with Being at the same time. It is a sensuous full-bodied presence – a baby walking like a Sumo wrestler. Sometimes Tibetan Lamas in their maroon robes embody this quality. The Pearl Essence is the radiance of Being in the body. There is a powerful kinesthetic awareness in the Pearl Essence. In it we are totally connected to Being and to the body.

The Pearl is our Buddha nature.

There is realness, simplicity and connectedness to the Pearl Essence. The Pearl represents Autonomy, a sense of individuality and independence that is totally connected to others - independent but not isolated. In the experience of the Pearl Essence, there is no need for pretense, drama or bullshit. The Zen saying "When we're hungry we eat" expresses it perfectly. We know where we are and what we're doing here. We emerge as an individual, but we belong to the world. We are our own person standing firmly on our own two feet. We are totally in touch with our skills and the resources of our personality. We can meet the other in our full presence. The Pearl is the capacity to be autonomous and to bond with others.

The ego is the grain of sand that allows the Pearl to unfold. It is in the unfolding of the Pearl Essence that the aware ego begins to emerge. Each stage of childhood adds another layer of the Pearl. Each quality of Essence we experience on our life journey adds another dimension to the Pearl Essence. The integration of the Pearl Essence brings ego efficiency and ego awareness. It facilitates a freely functioning ego. The Pearl Essence is about functionality - functioning from Essence rather than from fixation. The natural functions of the ego are enhanced and there is more harmony between the different parts of our ego. We are aware of our personality resources and they are fully available to us. We are also aware of our conditioning, our ego structure and our limitations. We have a clear sense of our capacities and what is needed in each situation. The different qualities of Essence spontaneously arise in the appropriate situations. The Pearl Essence is the capacity to integrate and digest the experiences of life as they are happening. We start to live life more fully in each moment. There is balance between our inner feelings and our outer activity. Our actions are informed by Being.

With the maturing of the Pearl Essence we no longer dissolve or self-destruct. We embody Being. We have a resilient ego that functions and integrates at the same time. We integrate our essential qualities through action. We create intimate relationships in which there is neither domination nor submission. We have clear but flexible boundaries and limits. In our actions there is presence, full awareness in the here and now. We become our own person, a distinct differentiated self, and we are intimately connected to others. We become psychologically and spiritually mature. There is more and more identification with Essence and less identification with ego.

In the West, the symbol for the Pearl is the Renaissance man who has mastered a wide variety of knowledge, arts and disciplines. In the East, the symbol for this quality is Krishna, the multidimensional, multicolored incarnation of Vishnu. He embodies all the qualities of Essence, appearing in many different incarnations. Master and teacher of all the yogas and the arts, Krishna is the divine union of Being and worldly action. He embodies the Pearl Essence as the integration of autonomy and intimacy, the lover and the warrior. In literature, he is the divine charioteer and the divine lover. Besides Radha, his consort, he has 16,000 wives, which also makes him the ultimate phallic narcissist.

The Pearl Essence is connected to all the stages of childhood and the integration of those stages. But the childhood stage of rapprochement is especially crucial to the development of the Pearl. This is the rapprochement stage of exploration and integration that lasts roughly from 18 months to three years of age. The rapprochement stage represents the child's first attempts to integrate its needs for intimacy and autonomy. Maturity depends on the integration of these two core needs - and that process of integration goes on throughout our lives.

THE PERFORMER FIXATION

Performers are generally energetic, cheerful, industrious, optimistic, persuasive and practical. They are the dynamic doers of the Enneagram. They are supremely confident and charismatic. The difficulty is that Performers feel deficient in their doing, in their Autonomy, and it frequently separates them from the Pearl Essence. Their doing is never enough. So they feel they have to do more, even though they are already doing a lot. Disconnected from Essence, Threes get swept away by their activities and become emotionally disconnected from their actions.

The activity of the Three personality is an attempt to embody the qualities of independence and maturity. It is also an attempt to get connection to others. "I have to produce in order to be loved," could express their core belief. In the family of Performers there was a lack of bonding between the different family members and Threes reacted to this deficiency with energetic, nonstop activity. They were rewarded primarily for what they accomplished. In the midst of all the doing and achieving, Performers lose the connection to themselves. So even though Threes are at the center of the feeling types, they often don't know what they feel.

Threes value competence. They seek recognition for what they do, for what they produce, for getting the job done. Unlike Givers, who seek recognition for what they do for others, Performers want to be appreciated for being competent, productive and professional. Unlike the Romantic number Four, who seeks recognition for their deep feelings and sensitivity, Threes want to be seen as the living embodiment of success. They want to be seen as an ideal, a prototype.

For Performers, living up to the grandeur of their self-images is often a burden. The performance eventually drains their emotional energy. Self-Image and idealized images of self play an extremely important role in understanding the Performer. The Performer is trying to project an image that is more akin to a prototype than a human being. The need to be seen as an iconic figure of competence and success takes an enormous amount of energy and frequently exhausts them. For some Threes, this drive goes in the direction of the phallic narcissist, the supreme seducer or seductress. They are making themselves into the most attractive, most admired beings on earth. They want recognition for being great lovers. There is a lot of competition with same-sex rivals and a lot of genital anxiety in their efforts to prove how great they are. The Three pre-occupation with image and looking good hides a deep sense of shame and unworthiness. The shame of the Three is especially connected to ego deficiency (see Chapter 1) and the gap they feel between their inner reality and their self-image.

Threes are supreme marketers. The product they are marketing is themselves, their idealized self-image. Self-promotion is the name of the game. Performers are showing how good they are by getting the job done. The emphasis is on speed and making things happen. They are chameleons who keep changing the image they are projecting while at the same time giving their total energy to making that image attractive to others. It is a very good performance – regardless of what image they are promoting. And there is invariably an element of deception and fictitiousness in it. Threes are never quite what they are billed to be. At the core of their self-marketing, their compulsive activity and their many achievements, Performers often feel like an empty shell.

The Performer fixation is an imitation of the Pearl Essence. Although Threes are attempting to project maturity, what they frequently embody is extreme immaturity. Their competitiveness and devotion to image, rather than substance, gives them an adolescent feel. They often look and act like teenagers even at an advanced age. Although they are striving for independence and autonomy, they live in an extreme codependence, under constant pressure to perform in order to get love and recognition from others. Deep down they often feel helpless, exhausted and isolated.

The heart and pericardium, the thin membrane that surrounds the heart, are the organs of importance for the Three. The Performer can be viewed as a disconnection from the heart. It is almost as if the pericardium has become metallic or hard in some way. The heart center becomes blocked and brittle, unable to really feel or to circulate emotional nourishment in the system. Threes often have this undernourished, worn out aspect, the result of a disconnection from the heart. They are prone to stress, exhaustion and heart disease.

MEETING THE PERFORMER IN OURSELVES

Extremely active periods in our lives will put us in contact with the Performer in us. Starting a business, raising a family or working more than one job can give us an experience of the Performer too. Whenever we feel intense pressure to be seen in a certain way, to be a success or to make significant achievements in a short span of time, we meet the Performer. The Performer fixation is an inner pressure to live up to a certain image of ourselves, and the image may be constantly changing. In the Performer fixation, we meet our roles and the gap between our inner reality and our mask. The image we are attempting to project becomes a tremendous weight because there is a lack of congruency between what is going on inside of us and the image we are projecting on the outside. There is often anxiety and agitation in our activity, which is highly focused on results and recognition. Sales and marketing professions generally experience this more than other professions. We get so involved in the nonstop doing that we do not realize how disconnected we are from ourselves. Though we are relating like crazy, there is a feeling of isolation in our intense activity.

NARCISSISM

Narcissism is alienation from our essential self, from who we really are. It is alienation from Essence. In the grip of our narcissism, we are identified with self-representations that separate us from a direct, intimate experience of ourselves. Narcissism represents an estrangement from our true nature. This separation from who we really are takes many forms. It can manifest as the absence of value and self-esteem or as narcissistic vulnerability, the tendency to feel hurt, slighted, or humiliated by the slightest lack of attention, approval or admiration. Grandiosity and idealization are also components of our narcissism. We inflate ourselves with imaginary qualities or idealize special others in order to give ourselves value. And we are confronted by our narcissistic vulnerability – reality can always bring us down. We are confronted by the failure of our ego activity and the poverty and emptiness of our inner life. Hopelessness, meaninglessness and depression are often products of our narcissistic wound.

We have a fundamental need for mirroring. We need to be seen, recognized and appreciated. In childhood we generally do not get mirrored or appreciated for our inner beauty, our radiance and our essential qualities. We get appreciation for how we look, what we wear, how good we perform certain tasks, how well we behave and so on. In short, we are appreciated for what is superficial. The result is that we identify with what is superficial – our clothes, our possessions, our behavior, our looks and so on - rather than with Essence or Being. This lack of mirroring at the essential level also creates in us a tremendous craving for recognition.

Enneatypes Two, Three and Four are powerfully involved in trying to get recognition through their false self-images. The result is unhealthy and unconscious expressions of narcissism. All the nine types of the Enneagram, however, are narcissistic in the sense that they all crave recognition for something, even if that need is primarily unconscious. We all have a need for essential mirroring. The sad truth is that we never got enough of being seen in our Essence, we never got enough of being seen for who we really are. And our narcissistic need often remains one of the most disruptive unfulfilled needs we carry inside of us.

INTEGRATING THE PEARL ESSENCE

To really integrate the Pearl Essence we need to realize that our separation from mother was both difficult and incomplete. The hidden anxiety around separation from her - fearing to be cut off or rejected, smothered or overprotected, controlled or manipulated – prevented us from really separating. In our adult lives fear of losing love stops us from individuating. One result is that we often think that standing up for ourselves means walking away from others. Unfortunately we never walk away from our object relations with mom. We still feel needy and deficient in relation to her and we are carrying that anxiety inside. There is conflict in our relationships because of the push-pull relationship we have between intimacy and autonomy.

So the first step toward integrating the Pearl Essence is to explore our fears of separation. We are still attached and needy in relation to mom. This may mean facing our fears of losing the Gold Essence or experiencing the discomfort of negative merging. It may mean facing the over-connection to mother and the lack of freedom of action we experience inside ourselves. It may mean facing the reactive, rebellious side of us that gets played out in our relationships. We need to acknowledge that we're still trying to get separate from mom and that our relationships suffer because of this. Our anxieties around separation from mother prevent us from growing up and living our truth in the world. We need to continue to do the work of integrating intimacy and autonomy in our lives.

The second step toward integration of the Pearl is coming to

terms with our ego. On the one hand we need a healthy ego structure in order to function. Weaknesses in our ego structure will
make the integration of the Pearl Essence more difficult. We
need stability in ourselves. On the other hand, we need to realize
that ego is a deficient reality. In Buddhist terms, there is "no
self-existent I". Our identification with ego and ego activity is
maya (illusion) produced by the combined effect of the senses
(*skandas*). In psychological terms, our sense of self is based on our
object relations and the feelings we generate in relation to others
(mostly our primary caretakers). In either case, there is a deep
insecurity in our identification with ego, both in our sense of self
and our sense of individuality. The basic state of the ego is
deficiency and insecurity, especially in relation to Being.

Basic ego functions facilitate our autonomy. These functions
include our capacity for language and thinking, our capacity to
organize and regulate, our capacity to make decisions and control
drives. But the development of ego structure does not necessarily
result in maturity. The integration of Essence, and the Pearl
Essence in particular, seems to be a prerequisite for maturity.
Integrating Essence and developing an aware ego are a single
process. The integration of the Pearl Essence implies an aware ego.
This means we are aware of the limitations of our ego and that we
also have the capacity to survive, adapt and grow. As we integrate
the Pearl Essence, we become more and more aligned with Essence
and less identified with ego activity and fixation.

Our true nature is Essence. As the Pearl Essence matures in us,
we are capable of meeting reality in a natural way. The Pearl
Essence is multidimensional – it implies the integration of all the
qualities of Essence. The Pearl is ego awareness and the capacity

to contain. We can contain and hold energy, both negative and positive. We can contain our frustration as well as our joy and bliss. There is no need to defend the old self, the old identifications with ego. The Pearl Essence means that we consciously support our contact with all the qualities of Essence, nurturing our resources and capacities in every way we can. Rather than defending the old sense of self, we support Essence in ourselves and in others. We become more and more mature, differentiated and autonomous because that is our true nature.

HEALING THE PERFORMER

For Performers, the healing often starts when they begin to recognize that there's a gap between their inner reality and the image they are trying to project. They need to begin to see the distinction between action that is connected only to ego image and role-playing, and action that is connected to the heart and belly. They need to begin to distinguish between fake pearls and real pearls. The Performer needs to clearly experience the difference between authentic action and action that is emotionally disconnected. For Threes, self-marketing and self-promotion easily become self-deception and lying. When Threes begin to realize how completely lost they are in their activity, how completely disconnected they are from their own actions - there is the possibility for them to start becoming aware of their fixation. They also need to become aware of the tremendous pressure they are under to accomplish, achieve and succeed – and how frantic they become under that pressure. They need to ease up on the non-stop doing.

One of the difficulties for Threes is that when they relax they start to feel fear. Non-doing brings with it the fear and panic of disintegration. There is a genital anxiety behind the hyperactivity of the Three that keeps them agitated and anxious. When they relax the doing they feel this genital anxiety. The fear is that without the performance they will lose the connection to others, they will lose the love. Performers need to see the fears that are driving their performance in order to relax it. They need to start facing their fears more directly and more honestly and sharing those fears with others. This can be part of a process of allowing more vulnerability in their intimate relationships.

Threes also need to begin to face the shame and unworthiness they feel deep inside. They are in a constant process of having to pump themselves up. Behind that activity there is a deep sense of unworthiness that they need to confront in themselves. Action, generating and role-playing are ways of avoiding feelings of shame. The whole Performer fixation can be regarded as a response to a deep sense of shame. Emotional work can be helpful for allowing Threes to get in touch with the roots of their feelings of shame and to heal them. A committed long-term relationship is often very healing for the Performer. A strong commitment to therapy can also be the door to healing Threes and to making the Pearl Essence a reality in their lives.

The Pearl Essence solves and heals the Three fixation, allowing Threes to come out of the stress of doing and performing, the stress of winning admiration from others. But there are two other Essences, both connected to the Enneatype Six, which are also important to healing the Three. The first is the Will Essence, which brings a sense of solidity, inner support, confidence and at-ease-ness. With the presence of the White Essence, Threes no longer feel the need to compete and prove they are the best. They feel solid enough to face their fears and anxieties. Inner Commitment is a secondary Essence connected to Enneatype Six. Inner Commitment is an aspect of Will that helps to anchor us in our truth and our spiritual path. We walk our walk. It also helps to release the defensive structures in us. The experience of Inner Commitment releases our survival fears. It helps to free Threes from the tendency to go for money and for goals based only on survival needs.

LEADERSHIP AND ORGANIZATIONS

Performers are hardworking go-getters who are usually good decision-makers. Three organizations value commitment, efficiency and consistency. They go for what they want without looking too hard at all the alternatives or the risks. Tasks are generally well defined and goals are clear and precise. Like Threes, the Performer organizations know where they want to go and how to get there. These organizations function best when there are lots of performance rewards and lots of opportunity for advancement. They do not function well in slow bureaucratic environments that frustrate achievement. Three companies generally excel in marketing and responding to the demands of the market.

Enron, the energy conglomerate that went bankrupt in America, was a good example of a mismanaged Three organization. From a small Texas energy concern it became a world player in energy markets, pioneering energy as a commodity traded in the marketplace like other commodities. For six years in succession Enron was awarded "America's most innovative company" award by Fortune magazine. The company was bold and successful and going for it on all levels. The ruthless desire to succeed eventually produced dishonest accounting practices and criminal behavior that landed many senior officers of the company in jail. The powerful drive to maintain Enron's high-performance image led management to make decisions that brought on the demise of the company. Like the Three fixation, Enron began to experience the tremendous gap between its successful go-getter image and the inner workings of the company, which were in chaos.

WORKING WITH THREES

When you meet Threes for the first time, be well prepared, direct and enthusiastic. Don't waste their time – they are busy people. When working with Threes, show appreciation for their accomplishments and give them the opportunity to excel. Never ignore or diminish their many achievements – it deflates them. Recognition and praise motivates them. Give them the space to express themselves, to open up to their deeper feelings. If your client is a Performer, demonstrate how your product will help them to be noticed and to show off their status or success.

COLLECTIVE EXPRESSIONS OF THE PERFORMER

The archetypal Three country is the United States. The American dream is a Performer dream of rags to riches, of unending accomplishments, of getting the job done no matter what. The present is sacrificed for the golden future. Success and fame are idealized and the ability to successfully market oneself is king. Collectively speaking, Americans know what they want and they go for it. Identification with idealized self-images motivates their drive for success and also guarantees their disconnection from who they actually are.

America represents the extraverted self. Americans often seem superficial and immature through the eyes of other cultures. They are under tremendous time pressure and pressure to perform. The outer, material, phenomenal reality has so much value and importance that the awareness of an inner reality frequently gets lost. In many Americans, there is often no awareness that such an inner reality exists. The loss of connection to self often goes unnoticed. The powerful imbalance between compulsive doing and a sense of being totally lost gives American society a rootless, adolescent, surreal feeling that is unique to it.

The image Americans promote to others is that of the prototype. Americans really do think that the rest of the world idolizes them and wants to be like them. And the steady flow of immigrants supports this illusion. Often their self-image is an inflated or a perfectionist image that is very far from their personal reality. Americans are narcissistic in the sense that they fall in love with their own self-image and then try to sell it to others. They often have a lot of difficulty "getting real" because there is so much involvement with their unreal, idealized images of themselves. Collectively Americans still tend to see themselves as good guys, their country a model for the rest of the world. The image Americans carry of themselves and their country, however, is wildly out of sync with the litany of horrors America has visited on the rest of the world, from Nicaragua to Chile, from Vietnam to Iraq. This distorted self-image is also out of sync with the long list of social, political and economic ills that afflict American society.

It is interesting to note that Enneatype Three was the only Enneagram type that was omitted from the DSM III (the psychiatric diagnostic manual). The easiest explanation for this omission is that Americans see the Performer personality as normal - as ideal, in fact.

CHAPTER 4

BELOVED OF THE HEART
ENNEATYPE 4

Name: The Romantic (Artist, Individualist)

Essence: True Self (inner light, point of light)

Color: Rainbow (all colors)

Symbol: The Beloved

Passion: Envy

Fixation: Melancholy, sadness

Psychology: Depressive

Family Deficiency: Lack of sense of self

Ego Ideal: Authenticity

Ego Confusion: Confuses the True Self (Rainbow Essence) with
dramatic feelings, self-obsession and being special

Mask: Always authentic, always deep

Specific Reaction: Inner control of self-image

Organs Affected: Lungs, diaphragm

THE RAINBOW ESSENCE

The Rainbow Essence is our essential identity. When we integrate the Rainbow Essence, we know who we are and we stop trying to find ourselves. We have a simple, direct experience of ourselves.

This quality ends the search for self. We are the light, we are Essence. In touch with this inner light, we glow in the different qualities of Essence. We are radiant. Rumi's words about Shems-e-Tabrizi, the wandering mystic who captured his heart, express it well: "There has never been such a one as you. You are the soul of the soul of the whirling dance." The Rainbow Essence is the Essence of our soul. Falling in love helps us to experience this quality and to see it in others. When we are in touch with the Rainbow Essence, we feel we are truly ourselves. Our essential self has a transparency that facilitates contact with all the qualities of Essence. It is a lightness of the heart. It is the joyful inner light that shines from the child's eyes, from the lover's eyes. It is the wonder of a star shining in the darkest night.

The Rainbow Essence is an expression of personal Essence, personal light. The Absolute is an expression of impersonal Essence, divine light. In terms of Essence, Christ's statement "I am the son of God" means I am the individuated light of the Absolute. Christ has a powerful inner light and he has powerful experiences of the different qualities of Essence. Al Hilaj Mansur's "Ana al Haq" (I am the Truth) expresses a similar relationship to the divine. In terms of Essence, Mansur's statement means I am the individuated expression of the truth of the Absolute. The True Self is our essential presence. Without this inner light, there is deadness in the soul. In the Rainbow Essence, we are the living presence of the divine.

The Rainbow Essence is our higher self, our True Self, the light of our soul. In our original nature, we are the light. We are the Heavenly Twin, we are the Beloved of the heart. Unlike the Pearl Essence, the Rainbow Essence is not about manifestation. It is about Being. It is about presence. It is self-realization in the sense that we realize who we are. We feel we are truly ourselves, in touch with all the qualities of Essence. The lover switches on this inner light in us. The Rainbow Essence brings us delight, joy and a childlike sense of wonder. We light up when the inner light is there. Children light up when we acknowledge this quality in them.

The Rainbow Essence activates other qualities of Essence, depending on where it is in the body. It is often experienced in the heart as overflowing love, but it is not limited in its expression. The True Self is an entity that is not static nor fixed. It is what leaves the body when we die. The Rainbow Essence brings with it an intrinsic sense of self. "I am a being of light dwelling in this beloved flesh," accurately expresses this truth of who we are.

THE ROMANTIC FIXATION

In touch with the True Self, Fours are compassionate, creative, inspired, expressive, intuitive, playful and lively. Disconnected from the Rainbow Essence, Romantics are moody, temperamental, self-pitying, depressive, envious, spiteful and self-absorbed.

The Romantic number Four is on a quest for the True Self, the Rainbow Essence. Don Quixote is a good example of this search of the romantic dreamer for a lost sense of self. The Romantic fixation represents alienation from self, alienation from the light. It is the alienation of the ego trying to be the light. We have strong experiences of the Rainbow Essence in childhood, especially during the practicing period (12-18 months of age) when we are filled with the delight and wonder of ourselves. But those experiences of inner light become more rare as we move through the stages of childhood. Our story becomes the story of a fallen being – Satan, Lucifer, Mephistopheles – the Beloved cast out of heaven. We were all beings of light but we got contracted and diminished, dulled by our conditioning, our society and our family environment. We got split off from our True Self, from who we really are. The Romantic is obsessed by this separation from the Rainbow Essence and the need to recover this quality.

The Romantic can be viewed as an introverted response to shame. From the outside Fours can appear refined, aloof, elegant and artistic, but the core feeling from childhood is rejection and abandonment, the feeling that something is drastically wrong with them. The resulting sense of shame is dealt with by being very original, creative, artistic or unique. Fours try to generate the Rainbow Essence through deep feelings. They seek recognition for their deep feelings and sensitivity. Being unique or special is a way of covering up the core feeling that they are tragically flawed. By indulging in emotions of pain, sadness, melancholy, and loss, Fours think they can produce the Rainbow Essence, but all they are creating is more frustration and false personality.

In childhood their idealized image of the True Self gave Fours a constant feeling of being flawed. As adults, Fours tend to hold a static image of the True Self that gets in the way of actually experiencing it. They become involved in controlling their own self-image in a way that makes them feel false. Their attempts to be authentic, to be true to themselves, result in an inner feeling of falseness. Fours rarely experience a stable sense of self and they usually feel some level of separation from the True Self. Hence there is a constant involvement in trying to be authentic, in generating a real sense of self.

Romantics create powerful feelings of envy in themselves. Comparison and envy ravage Fours. Often they project their inner light onto others, feeling that everyone has the inner light except them. They tend to implode and collapse, often feeling sorry for themselves. Experiencing problems or emotional dramas is their way to draw attention to themselves and a way to feel authentic. Suffering has a high value for them and unconsciously they take pleasure in it. Fours literally feel cast out of heaven. They often see themselves as being too different from their parents. The family constellation leaves them with a feeling of being eternal outsiders or aliens. Fours sometimes look like self-frustrating masochists filled with envy for what others have. They have a hard time moving toward what actually nourishes them. Like Quixote, they prefer to stay in the romantic dream rather than in its fulfillment. Their inner world is filled with a lot of fantasy, nostalgia and sentimentality, often going toward depression and thoughts of suicide.

Fours are love addicts, because love is the one thing that can put them directly in touch with the True Self. They are part of the Feeling Types, along with the Performer and the Giver, and they share not only their sense of shame but also their hunger for recognition. Because they often feel disconnected from the Rainbow Essence, Fours have to constantly prop up their self-image. All the emotional drama of the Romantic is an attempt to experience the Rainbow Essence, to be the inner light. All their attempts to be authentic and deep, however, just produce more false personality. Fours truly are tragic in the sense that they tend to live much of their lives in unfulfilled dreams, melancholy, heartache and sadness.

MEETING THE ROMANTIC IN OURSELVES

When we experience relationship crises such as divorce or dramatic separation, we are often thrown into the Four fixation. We may feel like we have lost the inner light forever and lost our sense of self. Or we may start to idealize the past and abhor the present. Sentimentality, self-pity and a sense of loss can dominate us in these times. When we meet others, we tend to bring them down. We feel lost in the darkness of our emotional turmoil.

When we attempt to appear special or elite in some way, we also start to meet the Four fixation in ourselves. Basically we start to act in ways that are supposed to reflect deep inner qualities. We try to separate ourselves from the crowd and make ourselves special. We may feel the need to appear very sensitive or artistic, or very trendy and stylish. The ego masquerades as the inner light, as the essential self, and there is a self-absorbed quality to our actions.

EGO MISSION AND FAMILY DEFICIENCY

The ego is on a mission. The mission is to produce something that was missing in the original family. For example, if the family was very poor, having few financial resources, the ego of the child might develop the mission to get rich. The ego mission is linked to a quality that was severely limited or absent in the original family. As children we sense what is missing in the family and we want to answer that need in order to rescue the family. The ego, like a small child, tries to generate this quality in order to get the love and attention of the parents. At the core of all our desires – this quality is present. Our ego idealizes this quality. This is the quality that will fix everything. This is the quality around which our fixation takes form.

Part of our ego formation also takes place around this essential quality that was missing in the family. Our ego tries to produce the missing quality. In the case of Enneatype One, it is the Pink Essence that was missing in the family, Perfect Love. The child is unconsciously aware that something is missing in the family system and unconsciously tries to rescue the family – by producing this missing quality. This becomes the ego mission of the Perfectionist – trying to get love by generating this missing quality. By being perfect, Perfectionists think they can produce the Pink Essence, heal the family and receive the love and appreciation they deserve. Their ego activity is motivated by a desire to recover Essence.

The reality is that our ego activity separates us from Essence and usually leaves us with a sense of failure. The desired outcome never really arrives. We don't rescue the family and we don't get the love and recognition we desire. Ego activity cannot produce Essence. Our ego activity has a good intention but the mission ends in failure. More importantly, the ego does not know exactly what it is trying to produce. It is a quality that was deficient or absent in the family even before our ego was formed. The ego is more familiar with the family deficiency, the absence of this essential quality, than with the quality itself. In a certain sense, the ego is groping in the dark for this quality that will rescue the family.

In the family of the Romantic there is a deficient sense of self. This can take many forms. For example, the parents are in very rigid roles that hide their deficient sense of self. Or the roles the parents are in are exaggerated and unreal, acted out for the benefit of others. The parents of Fours are often very narcissistic, very disconnected from any sense of the True Self. One way or another, the parents are compensating for the absence of any real sense of self. The Four child picks up on this family deficiency and starts to produce something that resembles an authentic sense of self. This is the birth of the Romantic fixation.

The importance of the ego mission is that we spend much of our lifetime consciously or unconsciously trying to fix the family we grew up in. We devote a lot of energy to producing something that was a response to the family need at a particular moment in its history, but which has no relevance to what we need to be doing in our lives now. In this way the ego mission sidetracks us from our real mission in life. Our soul is here for a specific purpose and we need to get in touch with what that is. The ego mission impedes the fulfilling of our soul mission. As we become more aware of our ego mission, we can start to let go of it and direct more attention to knowing and fulfilling our soul purpose.

INTEGRATING THE RAINBOW ESSENCE

In order to integrate the Rainbow Essence we need to examine our deep involvement in trying to fix our original family. The family deficiency, what was missing in the family at the time of our birth, is the obsession of our ego. In this way, our ego goes on trying to produce something that was needed in the distant past. We want to fill the family deficiency, rescue the family, heal the family - in order to get the inner light, in order to be the star, in order to be seen, loved and appreciated. Unconsciously we think that this is how to recover the Rainbow Essence. But we lose contact with the light and with our True Self in our ego activity. Filling the family deficiency dulls us and robs us of our dignity. The Rainbow Essence restores us to health and virtue.

So the more we clear up the family mess, our family constellation, the more crystallized our soul mission becomes. This supports the integration of the True Self. The Rainbow Essence, like the other qualities of Essence, helps to dismantle the fixated, obsessive energy of our ego. Ego is necessary for our capacity to function, but its repetitive activities lead us astray. The power of the ego mission in particular detours us from what we really need to accomplish in this life. It causes a deviation in our character, away from Essence and soul purpose, toward compulsive activity. At the core of our ego, lies the search for self. And the experience of the True Self ends that search. As we stabilize in our essential identity, our soul mission becomes more and more clear.

The Rainbow Essence is an inward orientation that takes us toward the light, toward real presence. This presence is a simple and direct experience of ourselves rather than a movement outward toward what is illusion and unreality. Knowing our soul purpose is part of this orientation toward what is real. Our soul is here in this earthly plane to accomplish something. And there may be several soul missions in us. When one soul mission is fulfilled, others may also arise. But knowing our soul purpose gives us a tremendous sense of inner stability, perseverance and strength. Being aligned with our soul purpose gives us a resolute diamond-like sense of inner directedness that helps to integrate the Rainbow Essence, the

True Self. We know who we are in a very clear, powerful way.

One reason the narcissistic drive is so powerful in us is because we haven't found the inner light, True Self, the star of Being. We haven't found out who we really are. By exploring the issues of our narcissism, we liberate the inner light. As the Rainbow Essence begins to stabilize in us, we no longer need to prove we are special. The distortions of narcissism start to diminish. The grandiosity, self-inflation and posturing that reflect our narcissistic wound start to dissolve, as do the hopelessness and the despair. We start to let go of the false self-images we carry inside of us. We no longer feel enraged about not being seen in our Essence or our light. We no longer feel betrayed by the loss of self, the loss of Essence that accompanied our childhood. We know that we are the Beloved. We are that star shining in the darkest night.

Working with the emotional child, the wounded inner child, is generally not a way to integrate the True Self. By working with the emotional child we can know our wounds, but we cannot find the inner light. The child part of us that is more appropriately connected to the Rainbow Essence is the magical child. The magical child, bubbling with essential qualities, is more closely connected to who we really are. The magical child is full of wonder, majesty and enchantment. The magical child represents our childhood experiences of Essence and our essential self. This is the child part of us that needs to be integrated into our adult self.

HEALING THE ROMANTIC

The key to healing for the Romantic is for them to experience fully the truth that all their melancholy, sadness and inner drama has nothing to do with the Rainbow Essence. Their tragic inner reality needs to be seen as an exaggeration, a self-defeating indulgence in false personality and sentimentality. Fours need to experience the deeper feelings that live beneath their emotional dramas. Once Fours have experienced how much unnecessary pain and frustration they are creating in their lives, the Rainbow Essence starts to become more available. They begin to shine. Fours need to realize that they cannot get in touch with their inner light through ego activity. Because Fours idealize the True Self as a perfect sense of self, they think they have to be only in this Essence all the time. They need to acknowledge and accept the fact that they are sometimes disconnected from the Rainbow Essence. Then the activity of the ego can relax and the True Self can emerge.

Another aspect of the healing for Fours involves the disconnection from the Pink Essence, Perfect Love. The line between One and Four indicates this disowned Essence. Somehow Romantics turned their back on the Pink Essence, angrily rejecting the breast at some point in babyhood. This angry turning away is often a rejection of nourishment, of what they need most. Often Fours cut themselves off from what could really support them and nurture them. As adults, Fours seem to be turning away from the love and support that is available, while at the same time longing for what is unreachable or unavailable. They need to start turning their attention to the nourishment that is available here and now.

Fours need to stop getting lost in the emotional wilderness and to start directing themselves toward obtainable goals, toward action based on honest commitment, discipline and perseverance. Tragic Romantics need to stop giving up and collapsing in the emotional drama of their inner lives. The depth of their shame needs to be squarely faced and experienced. This can help them begin to appreciate their own beauty and creativity, without the pressure to prove they are unique or special. Fours need to start living a healthy narcissism that allows them to be seen and appreciated for who they are, not for some quality they are aspiring to embody. They need to realize that everything is available here and now, not in some imaginary realm of the past or future. The Romantic needs to stop living in unfulfilled dreams and to start living in what is available, what is real, what is possible. Dreams also come true.

Romantics think love is what is going to save them. Love gives them the experience of the Rainbow Essence. Often they project their inner light on others and fall desperately in love. They idealize the other and fall desperately in love with their idealization. This can be called "giving away the light," in a way that causes them great suffering and pain. The lover ends up with the light - and the Romantic ends up in darkness. Integrating the Rainbow Essence is what heals the Four and restores their emotional equilibrium, their damaged self-image and their love relationships.

LEADERSHIP AND ORGANIZATIONS

Fours motivate others by force of character. They inspire people to go to the heart of the matter, to the depths of their feelings. Once they emotionally understand what is needed, they go for it. They can be heroic and forceful in putting radical ideas into action. This can be energizing or frustrating for their employees. Though the Four leader may have a strong personal vision, they can often be inconsistent, moody and imperious. They are usually long on creativity and style, and short on practicality and attention to the bottom line. They want to fulfill their personal vision at all costs.

Four organizations often fill a special high-end niche in the marketplace. They mirror the elitist disposition of their leaders. They are not service oriented so much as they are quality and style driven. They strive to have a unique high-quality product that also demands a high price. Cartier, Tiffany, Chanel and Rolex are such organizations, with products to match. The best words to describe these organizations are special and specialist. Non-profit organizations are also frequently Four organizations, passionate about causes that involve human suffering and tragedy. Médecins Sans Frontières and Save the Children are good examples of these organizations.

WORKING WITH FOURS

Because they are emotionally volatile, Romantics need clear objectives, boundaries and performance criteria in their work environment. They function best when there is consistent management and plenty of space for their creativity. Fours need to feel valued for their creativity, their esthetic sensibilities, their deep insights and vision. They do not function well in tasks they deem mundane or superficial. They need to be appreciated for their sense of style and innovation. Fours are very original. Even though they are sensitive and empathic, Fours are not easy to get along with and they generally do not have an easy time with relating. Never challenge the depth of their feelings or their authenticity. To tell a Four that they are false or superficial in some way will provoke the ultimate reaction, be it rage or depression. Never challenge directly their views on matters of style and taste. Make them feel unique and special. Avoid loud, aggressive or exaggerated behavior. Respect their moods and the sanctity of their unique work environment.

COLLECTIVE EXPRESSIONS OF THE ROMANTIC

Russia is the ultimate Four country. Anna Karenina and Dr. Zhivago represent this highly tragic and highly romantic predisposition of the Russian collective. Russia has soul. Heart and soul. And love is always tragic in some way. The hopeless love affairs that end in suicide are idealized. Mayakovsky, a writer whose life mirrored this tragedy of lost love and suicide, is an icon of the tragic Russian collective and its tragic past. Poetry and music and the expression of deep feelings are the domain of all Russians. They are not reserved just for the poets and artists. Russian women have a special place in the pantheon of female beauty because they are often very alive in the Rainbow Essence or in glittery imitations of it. Russians love what is refined, elegant and elitist, despite their long communist past, which attempted to eradicate these bourgeois tendencies. Flamboyant, eccentric behavior has a high value and is generally admired, as does anything done in the name of love.

The Arab world is in general a romantic world of the Four. Some Arab countries - such as Algeria, which is an Eight country – fall into other fixations. But most Arab countries are solidly in the mould of the Romantic number Four. Very poetic and artistic, highly emotional, they produce great spiritual seekers, poets and musicians. Om Kalthoum, the legendary Egyptian singer, used to produce tremendous outpourings of emotion when she sang for large audiences. The Sufis are a uniquely Four expression of spirituality. There is tremendous longing in the Arab collective for the past, for the lost golden age of Islam - and a tremendous resistance to modernity. Because the Arab world has generally not had an easy time in adapting to the modern world, there is also frustration and envy in the collective. There is narcissistic rage and resentment in many Arab countries at not having been able to take their rightful place in the world.

Romantic love is very present in the poetry and literature of the Arab world. *Layla* and *Majnun*, the story of two lovers who are prevented from meeting but intensely feel each other's love and pain, is one of the great love stories of the Arab world. The longing for love, for what is unavailable, what has been lost or what could have been – these are all hallmarks of the Four fixation and the Arab world. There is a powerful identification with the impossible love affair, the longing for a dream that can never come true.

CHAPTER 5

DIVINE LIGHT
ENNEATYPE 5

Name: The Observer (Thinker, Miser)

Essence: Inner Guidance/Diamond Guidance

Color: Diamond

Symbol: Gautama Buddha

Passion: Greed

Fixation: Stinginess

Psychology: Schizoid, avoidant

Family Deficiency: Absence of guidance, absence of real
understanding

Ego Ideal: Omniscience

Ego Confusion: Confuses Inner Guidance (Diamond Essence)
with information, knowledge and intellectual activity

Mask: Always objective

Specific Reaction: Withdraw, disappear

Organs Affected: Solar plexus, hypothalamus gland

THE DIAMOND ESSENCE

Inner Guidance is about real understanding, real knowing that does
not come just from the head but from all three centers - belly, heart

and mind. It is as if a diamond descends inside of us and there is clarity and the capacity to know throughout the system. It is precise knowing at the essential level. Diamond Essence gives us the capacity to see the whole, the overview, the relationship between the different realms of existence. It is the capacity to explore in detail the different aspects of Essence. Diamond Guidance is the capacity to really know – especially to know our inner reality. It is this capacity that empowers our soul to develop and unfold. It gives us direct and precise knowing about the different realms and dimensions inside of us. Essence gets transformed into the capacity to understand on many different levels at the same time.

The Diamond Essence is a quality of the heart. For the Sufis, Inner Guidance sometimes appears as Kidr, the green one who speaks to the heart. Kidr is the inner voice or an inner knowing that enables us to act in ways that are beyond the mind, beyond our conscious understanding. We are guided by a source that is beyond the conventional dimension. In the Sufi tale of Mojud, the man with the inexplicable life, Kidr as the inner voice tells Mojud to jump in the river - and this act supports the dynamic spiritual development of his life. Mojud's life continues to change through the guidance of Kidr, in ways that are beyond his conscious understanding. Inner Guidance is essential guidance rather than the guidance of fixation and ego. Guidance dictated solely by the mind is linear and horizontal. Diamond Guidance is vertical and multidimensional, manifesting in all the dimensions of existence.

Inner Guidance is compassionate and stern. There is toughness and directness to this quality of guidance. Systems, religions, gurus and our devotion to them tend to block the

Diamond Guidance. They are the outer identification of ego, poor substitutes for real Inner Guidance. And we are led astray by these imitations of guidance. Gurus often play the role of the Diamond Guidance, but it is mostly the projections of their followers that give them this role. We need teachers, mentors and role models, but we also need to know that their truth is not our truth, their path is not our path. The outer teacher can only help to orient us toward the awareness and development of Inner Guidance. In the same way, the Essence model needs to be used to discover our own truth, our personal reality. We need to keep the focus on ourselves, on our personal development, not on the system, which is only a finger pointing the moon. The Enneagram is a very good tool, but it is just a tool.

The Diamond Guidance is inside of us at a very high level - at the level of Being, at the highest level of knowing. It can appear to us in many forms – as a wise old man or woman, as grace, as a voice, a feeling, a dream or an invitation. But normally it comes to us in our everyday experiences, in the form of our life situations, which test us and challenge us to develop spiritually and psychologically. The more we integrate the Inner Guidance, the more our external life situations become part of this dynamic process.

In Tibetan Buddhism, Inner Guidance is the quality of Prajna Paramita, discriminating wisdom or intelligence. In many languages of the East, the word for heart and mind are the same. Inner Guidance is wisdom in the form of an enlightened synthesis of understanding that evolves from both heart and mind. Prajna Paramita is associated with Avalokiteshvara (Tibetan Chenrezig) the goddess of compassion. It is wisdom that comes from the heart. This quality provides us with an accurate perception of reality, objective consciousness. The qualities of Essence and their functions can be seen clearly. We all have discriminating intelligence at the conventional level, at the level of intellect. Diamond Guidance is discriminating intelligence at the level of Being, an accurate discerning of the direction of the soul. It is the fundamental quality for exploring our inner reality and for expressing and actualizing this reality in our daily life. The Diamond Guidance helps us to discriminate between what works and what doesn't in this process. It helps us to move naturally in the direction of spiritual and psychological health. The Diamond Essence empowers the soul to unfold and develop.

Diamond Guidance can manifest through us in many ways. It is a knowing that is alive to the moment. We tell jokes when jokes are needed, we get angry when anger is needed. By responding out of the moment in ways that often go against what we think should happen, we are also able to transmit this quality to others. When we find ourselves in a teaching role, Diamond Guidance enables insight, knowledge and analysis to function simultaneously together. In sports terminology, we are "in the zone". Our knowing functions independently of the conscious mind, just as the body of an athlete performs optimally without the involvement of the conscious mind. We can process and transmit essential understanding at the same time. We are in contact with both conceptual reality and essential reality. Being informs intellect, intellect informs Being.

Inner Guidance is not about surrendering to the will of God or to the Absolute, though it allows the Absolute to manifest through us. It doesn't mean putting everything in the hands of existence or in the hands of God. Inner Guidance needs discipline and taking responsibility on our part. We need to meditate to receive this kind of guidance. We need to work on ourselves in order to transmit this kind of knowing. We need to be committed to our inner journey and its unfolding, committed to the evolutionary inner force in us that needs to develop and manifest.

THE FIVE FIXATION

In contact with Essence, Fives are objective, perceptive, self-contained, persevering and intelligent. They are smart and generally very good in dealing with conceptual reality. They have the capacity to concentrate on complex issues and solve them. Disconnected from Essence they are intellectually arrogant, emotionally detached, cold, critical, unassertive and stingy. Disconnected from the Diamond Guidance, Fives tend to have a strong fear of not being competent, of not having enough expertise or knowledge to meet the challenges of life. Hence they always feel they need more information. This gives them an obsessive interest in information, knowledge and systems. They tend to isolate themselves inside the ivory tower of the mind, becoming emotionally distant and unavailable.

Along with Enneatypes Six and Seven, the Observer is a thinking type, a fear type. These three personality types can be viewed as three ways to deal with fear. They are all strong in the mind, in the mental body - and weak in the belly, in their guts. For the Observer, it is as if the emotional and instinctual centers have both been turned away from their original function in order to serve the mental body. All the energy gets channeled into the mind.

The Observer represents an introverted way of dealing with fear. In the Five family intellectual activity and knowledge were highly valued. The energy of the Five child was often too much for the parents and was channeled into mental activity. There was often a lack of maternal tenderness in the family that Observers compensated for by limiting their own needs. From the outside they often look miserly and stingy, especially in their care of themselves. They generally don't give themselves much. There is a strong sense of inner scarcity in Fives. Unconsciously Observers feel that the gathering and systematizing of information will eventually get them the nourishment that is so often lacking in their lives. Fives withdraw in order to feel safe but they are often highly undernourished, isolated and alone.

There is in the Observer a lack of juice, energy and lubrication in the nervous system and the emotional body. Social contact exhausts them. At parties Fives just run out of energy at some point and disappear. They have a core need of being alone in order to recharge and regenerate their resources. Basically the Observer always feels like a stranger, like they are not entirely welcome, that they need to hold back their energy, withdraw physically or disconnect emotionally in order to feel safe. Taking refuge in the mind is the result of a deep wound wherein Fives never felt supported in their own life energy. In the family system, Observers did not feel safe with either parent. Behind their isolating, avoidant behavior is the fear of engulfment, the fear of being overwhelmed or suffocated by the other.

The Observer confuses Inner Guidance with information, knowledge and intellectual activity. So there is pressure to get more information or analyze things down to smaller and smaller detail, in order to get guidance. But the Inner Guidance never arrives that way. Deep down Fives feel totally lost. They are often stuck in the mind and disconnected from their heart, their passion and their gut feelings. To others, it sometimes feels like Fives are disembodied, like the body is just a shell or a phantom, like the physical presence is missing in them. There is a continual sense of withholding in them, of pulling back or pulling up and out of the body. This is usually an attempt to get safe and to get an overview, omniscience. They do this by disconnecting from life, emotionally and physically, by distancing themselves from the messy crucible of life happening moment to moment. When you see Fives in groups they are often a little bit back and a little bit up - in order to get some distance from others and an overview of what is happening. They approach swimming (life) with only one foot in the water. Fives prefer a coaching role that experiences the game of life from the sidelines and loathes the thought of actually playing the game.

MEETING THE OBSERVER IN OURSELVES

Because so much of the modern world is functioning solely through the mental body, the mind or the intellect - we all have more and more opportunity to see the Observer in ourselves. When we get involved in projects that engage only the mind, disconnecting us from the emotions and the physical body, we start to meet the Five fixation in ourselves. This can mean losing ourselves in the gathering and systematizing of information. It can mean a life at the computer with little time for relationships or social contact. When we meet the Observer in ourselves and in others, we meet the new monks of the information age. In this very mental approach to life, we generally lose the path to our personal development and our spiritual unfolding. We lose touch with the needs of our soul.

THE METHODOLOGY OF RECOVERING ESSENCE

Conceptually the path to recovering and integrating Essence can be broken down into several distinct steps, but practically we do not travel the path to Essence in such a schematic, linear way.

Understanding how we integrate Essence means understanding the exploration of two dimensions of our personal reality – deficient emptiness and inner spaciousness. Our defenses and our ego activity in general are aimed at countering the uncomfortable feelings of deficient emptiness. When we relax our ego activity we start to feel the deficient emptiness, the feelings of not being good enough or not being okay. Exploring these feelings is the path to experiencing Essence. Inner spaciousness, on the other hand, is the presence of one or more qualities of Essence in us. The exploration of Essence may also lead to our difficulties with a particular quality, which will in turn bring up the deficient emptiness and how we defend against it. Like the play of shadow and light, there is constant movement inside of us between deficient emptiness and inner spaciousness (see Diagram C). We need to become more aware of this inner movement. Deficient emptiness will ultimately lead us to inner spaciousness, and inner spaciousness will also sometimes lead us to the deficient emptiness. As the Santana lyric renders it "There's a darkness living deep in my soul, it's still got a purpose to serve." Deficient emptiness does indeed have a purpose to serve – it is the vehicle through which we integrate Essence.

Often, but not always, the way to integrating Essence starts by our becoming aware of a pattern of thoughts, emotions or behaviors that is repeating in our lives. This pattern may be experienced as an emotional wound, a compulsion, a difficulty or a shortcoming. As we become more aware of the pattern, we begin to examine the issues that are connected to it. We explore the issues in whatever way we can – through individual sessions, personal inquiry, meditation and so forth. If the issues are extremely difficult for us we may need a psychotherapist to accompany us.

Since deficient emptiness is at the core of all our compulsive ego activity, we will naturally meet the ways we defend against this uncomfortable emptiness, the ways we defend against our feelings of not-enough-ness or not-okay-ness. It is this defending against deficient emptiness through incessant ego activity that is blocking Essence. The activity of defending is blocking our connection with Being. So we need to relax that activity and be in the deficient emptiness before a particular quality of Essence can arise. By exploring the issues connected to a certain quality, we relinquish some of our ego activity, feeling the discomfort or the pain that lies behind that activity.

As we allow ourselves to feel the deficient emptiness – and this may be experienced in many different ways, from tears to silent witnessing – our system unblocks, gaining more flexibility and flow. At this point we might begin to experience heat or other sensations in the body. This is a process where we begin to recover a particular quality of Essence that may have been buried for many years. When Essence begins to circulate in our system, we may feel clearer, more whole or more real. Or we may feel more present or more ordinary, more grounded or more relaxed. It depends on the quality of Essence we are exploring. And it may take several weeks or months for a particular quality of Essence to stabilize in us, depending on how much attention is needed in order to deal with the issues surrounding that Essence.

INTEGRATING THE DIAMOND ESSENCE

What blocks Inner Guidance is our arrogance, the feeling that we already know everything. It is our habitual mental and emotional habits - our preferences, our likes and dislikes - that bind us to the conventional dimension. Our fixation is dense and opaque – it obscures objective understanding. When we get out of our own way, the Diamond Essence can manifest. Specifically, this means that we become more transparent and permeable so that the light of understanding can come through us. J. Krishnamurti called this state of understanding "choiceless awareness". Osho called it "witnessing". But this is not a dissociated or detached kind of awareness. It is a fully alive presence that has the capacity to synthesize Being and conceptual knowledge in the moment. When Inner Guidance is there, like an older benevolent part of us, the ego can relax and let go of its repetitive activities. The Diamond Essence brings the light of understanding to the human realm.

As we mature in the work, Diamond Guidance replaces the superego, the critical self. The superego is basically a mechanical, reactive part of us. The superego helped us to survive in childhood but in adulthood it is mostly in our way. In particular, it hinders true guidance. The judgments of the superego often come with such force and aggression that they can paralyze us or cause us to collapse or to struggle against them. As we become more aware of this older part of us, the super ego softens and becomes more like a true friend. This allows the Diamond Essence to arise, to manifest in all the centers of the body, in all the dimensions of Essence. Our inner world starts to take the form of a diamond - a moment-to-moment clarity that is beyond knowing. So coming to terms with the superego - integrating it into our adult self or making friends with it - is very important. Otherwise this judgmental part of us functions like a punishing parent, infantilizing us and preventing us from realizing a mature sense of Inner Guidance.

In order for the Diamond Guidance to function we need to be open to our own experience of reality, including our personal reactions and preferences. This is an objectivity that implies a full personal contact with our own experience, with the field of existence in which we live. "Witnessing" does not mean that we are separate from our own experience. It means we are open to our own experience, to inquiring into it in a way that has heart and passion. The belief that we need to be dissociated from our own experience in order to understand it separates us from Inner Guidance. The belief that we need to be outside our own experience in order to understand it blocks the Diamond Essence. The synthesis of direct experiential understanding and conceptual understanding is what the Diamond Guidance is about. We need to be intimately in touch with our feelings, sensations, reactions and impulses in order to integrate the Diamond Essence. We cannot distance ourselves from full contact with the world, with other people, with life happening in its totality.

In order to fully integrate Inner Guidance in ourselves we need to become aware of all the ways in which we defend against guidance. Our resistance to real guidance comes in many forms - our mistrust, our preferences, our lack of orientation toward truth. Who cares about knowing the truth of our situation? Sometimes we want to go for emotional excitement instead of objective truth. Sometimes we don't want to be a witnessing consciousness. We need to examine our mistrust, our sense of betrayal, our feelings of being misguided and led astray by people we trusted. This will invariably bring us face to face with the shortcomings we experienced in the guidance of our parents. We need to look at the ways in which we devalue our intuition and our knowing. Probably no one ever guided us toward our soul mission or toward Being. Inner Guidance is one of the most challenging qualities of Essence. We need to work with all the issues of guidance in order to liberate its capacities.

HEALING THE OBSERVER

The Observer is yearning for real guidance. The absence of Inner Guidance in the Five is experienced as inner starvation, dryness, scarcity and emptiness. Diamond Guidance heals the whole system of the Observer, which is in enormous stress around knowing - trying to know everything and trying to get safe through knowing. Inner Guidance relaxes the Five and allows real understanding and guidance to arise. The Diamond Essence clears up misunderstandings around experiential knowledge and conceptual knowledge. When Fives realize that their activities around systems, knowledge and information gathering are futile attempts to get guidance, they start to relax. As the ego activity relaxes its grip on Observers, the Diamond Guidance becomes more and more available to them.

There is an original loss of Essence at the core of the Observer, a childhood disconnection from the Red Essence, which is Strength. This is represented by the line between Five and Eight on the Enneagram. Fives turned their backs on the vitality, the aliveness and turned-on-ness of the Red Essence. This Essence got diminished or blocked because the Five child often feared being too much for their parents. This turning away from Essence deeply wounded the Five. The visceral energy of the Red Essence got repressed in the Observer and resulted in a corresponding overvaluing of the mind and mental activity. The little energy bomb, the little Sumo wrestler that the Five was in childhood, got transformed into the cool aloof adult, taking refuge inside the mind. As children Fives turned their back on the aliveness and spontaneity of the Red Essence, amputating an essential part of themselves. At the core of the Five, there is usually a lot of rage connected to this loss of Essence. Fives need to access their rage and pain. Getting in touch with their anger and finding safe ways to express that anger may be part of this healing process.

Fives like to hang out in the impersonal or transpersonal qualities of Essence, especially the Absolute. But the personal qualities, such as the Rainbow Essence, the Red and the Gold Essence, are generally more difficult for Observers to access. So often the direction of healing for Fives lies in the integration of personal Essence.

LEADERSHIP AND ORGANIZATIONS

Five leaders like to make decisions and exercise control over their organization. They like to be in charge, but it is not a "hands on" style of control, but rather something that more resembles remote control. This is done through memos and written directives, affording little personal contact or guidance to their employees. Five leaders like to control information. Their authority usually comes from their knowledge and expertise. They are usually experts in some unique or specialized field. And the Five organization usually functions in areas of advanced technology. At their best Five leaders can be visionary, responsive to both employees and clients. At their worst, Five leaders can be paranoid and miserly, hoarding information and severely limiting creativity and communication within the organization.

The Five organization is an ivory tower of information. It is an information hierarchy. What you know often determines your status, power and importance. Five organizations can be extremely miserly, refusing to spend money in ways that hinder their effectiveness. Poor communication is a common difficulty in Five organizations. Casual socializing is discouraged, interpersonal contact is limited and there is a reliance on email and written communication – all of which contribute to the lack of effective communication. Five organizations are generally good in resolving complex technical problems and in paying attention to details.

WORKING WITH FIVES

Fives need to understand things through the mind first, through thinking and intellect. They need to be satisfied in the mind before they can begin to understand in other ways. So you need to approach them through the intellect first. Fives respond well to creative ideas, logic and factual or technical information. They resent boundary intrusions and are protective of their private space. Surprise visits are not welcomed, so make an appointment if you want to meet them. Create a safe and protective environment for meeting one-on-one with them. Be direct, precise and to the point in your meetings with them. They love to go into details, so give them the space to do that. Do not expect them to remain long in meetings, as it will exhaust them and cause them to withdraw more into themselves. Fives do well when they are given authority and responsibility and are challenged to act. They need to be encouraged to come out of the ivory tower of the mind and to take action.

COLLECTIVE EXPRESSIONS OF THE OBSERVER

To my knowledge there are no archetypal Five countries, but France comes closest to being in the Five fixation. The French are intellectually arrogant. Their approach to life is often emotionally detached and highly intellectual. Descartes' dictum "Je pense donc je suis" (I think therefore I am) still has a certain truth to it, namely the primacy of thinking and intellect. The French are generally more comfortable in the mental body than they are in either the physical or emotional body. The school system in France is primarily geared to producing intellectuals. The French have a weighty intellectual tradition and they enjoy analyzing things down to the last small detail. Despite the defeats and humiliations

France has suffered in its modern history - and they are many - the French still manage to be somewhat arrogant about their history and culture. There is a *hauteur* and a detachment in the French that reflects the Observer. And France itself has always maintained a separate status, slightly withdrawn from the community of nations, slightly superior, aloof and analytical - all in the style of the Five fixation.

Nevertheless, France also exhibits many tendencies of the Romantic fixation. The elitism of the ruling class is one of them. The French preoccupation with style, elegance and luxury items is also very much in the Four fixation. The same goes for the French devotion to the arts and their reverence for artists. If you listen to popular music in France, you will hear a lot of tragic love songs. Love and affective relationships in general are a strong preoccupation of the French. And there is often a lot of the sadness and melancholy of the Romantic fixation in these love stories. But even though there is considerable drama in intimate relationships in France, there is also much that is not dramatic. Often partners have intimate sexual relationships outside the couple and there is nothing particularly dramatic or exceptional about this state. Husbands have their mistresses, wives have their lovers, and life goes on – often without divorce. It is as though the temperament of the Romantic has been tempered by the intellect of the Observer.

CHAPTER 6

THE WAY OF THE WHITE CLOUDS
ENNEATYPE 6

Name: The Skeptic (Loyalist, Questioner, Devil's Advocate)

Essence: Will

Color: White

Symbol: Mount Kailash surrounded by white clouds

Passion: Fear

Fixation: Courage/cowardice

Psychology: Paranoid

Family Deficiency: Absence of safety or support

Ego Ideal: Strength, solidity

Ego Confusion: Confuses Will (White Essence) with defensiveness and counter-phobic activity

Mask: Always courageous

Specific Reaction: Defensive suspicion, mistrust

Organs Affected: Colon, kidneys

THE WHITE ESSENCE

The White Essence is a relaxed confidence that gives us the

capacity to trust and to surrender to what is. In contact with the Will Essence we feel grounded, centered, capable and at ease with challenges of life. There is an absence of effort, pushing and forcing things to go our way. The White Essence gives us a sense of confidence in the natural movement of life happening moment to moment. When present, the Will Essence enables us to give up control from the solar plexus. We can breathe deeply. In the experience of the White Essence there is a sense of inner support, inner strength that is rooted in our legs, our belly and our sex. We are in a state of release rather than a state of tension, stress and defensive contraction. We become more supple and flexible in our actions, and at the same time more solid and more rooted in our resolve. We possess an unshakable inner authority or inner confidence that is not rigid or fixated on outcomes. Our confidence is in ourselves, not in a specific outcome.

Determination and commitment are part of the White Essence. It is the commitment to stay open to our own experience, to go deeper. It is a willingness to go through the difficult places, the dark nights. Unwavering dedication and firm intention are needed to carry on the journey into our personal reality, into shadow and light, Essence and fixation, Being and deficiency. The color white implies purity, a purity of intention to stay the course, holding the tiller steady through both calm and stormy seas. The Will Essence is steadfastness. The purity of the White means we are not swept away by distractions or diversions. We don't give in to hopelessness and despair. We don't give in to seductive ways to go unconscious. We persevere. Our sense of inner support means we are grounded in our own experience. Inner support implies the understanding that we are solely responsible for our inner exploration, for discovering the truth within ourselves.

The White Essence can be powerful or delicate. It can be dense and solid or permeable and fluid. In the presence of the Will Essence there is love and friendliness, the real ability to support others. There is a deep relaxation and trust in existence. We have the energy to complete projects and get things done with ease and ordinariness. Life is not a big deal or a big threat or a big challenge. We are just very present, grounded, solid and realistic. We do what needs to be done. There is not a lot of excitation or wildness in our physical or psychological movements. We are not projecting incredible things onto others or onto the situations we meet from day to day. There is a smooth and steady flow to our life energy. We don't fight the river, we don't swim against the current.

The White Essence is the solid ground beneath our feet. We don't need to push ourselves because we are fully present here and now, solid on the earth, in the body and in ourselves. We are ready for whatever comes. We can move with the flow of existence and be solid in ourselves at the same time. We trust the movement of nature and of life. Like the mountain, we are steadfast and solid. Like the white clouds, we move effortlessly.

THE SIX FIXATION

In contact with Essence, Sixes are loyal, caring, practical, hard working, responsible, witty, compassionate, intuitive and energetic. They usually possess a lot of energy and creativity. Disconnected from Essence they are mistrustful, paranoid, reactive, suspicious, hyper-vigilant, tense and pessimistic. Disconnected from the Will Essence, Skeptics are fearful pushers who never feel secure and never relax.

Like the Planner and the Observer, the Skeptic is a fear type. Skeptics deal with their feelings of fear through unrelenting, charged mental activity. Fear actually energizes Sixes in an adrenaline-based, charging-up of the nervous system. In their comportment, Sixes may sometimes behave like immobilized couch potatoes, but the mind of the Six is very active and vigilant, on the lookout for possible threats. At the core of the Six, there is doubt, mistrust and dilemma. Should I or shouldn't I? Should I submit or rebel? Should I trust or not trust? There was an absence of safety in the childhood of the Skeptic that now keeps them busy with the issue of how to feel safe, and they deal with that issue primarily through thinking. The physical responses of the Six are more on the order of fight or flight. Counter-phobic Sixes want to fight, they want to confront others, so they can feel safe. The phobic Sixes tend be more social and submissive, while at the same time never relaxing their guard.

The family environment of the Six was unsafe - no one was there for anyone. Usually one parent was unreliable, undermining the child's trust. Or there was one parent who was often on the verge of exploding. Or there was a lot of conflict between the parents. There was no one the child could really trust or rely on. So the question for the Skeptic is how to get safe in the jungle reality of life. Everyone has a hidden agenda, no one is really trustworthy and there are always potential threats, real or imagined. Because of the feeling of lack of support on the inside, Sixes experience a lot of negative projection and paranoia. Often Skeptics are harboring unspoken negative thoughts and suspicions about others – and they imagine others are harboring the same negativity toward them.

Defensive suspiciousness, doubt and mistrust are the result.

Skeptics try to be strong, solid and dependable – but they cannot really do it. There is too much fear in the nervous system. They pretend to be tough when they really are not, especially the counter-phobic Sixes, who are sometimes leading the charge against an unjust authority. Counter-phobic Sixes are trying to prove they are not afraid, sometimes by taking on risky activities like mountain climbing or racecar driving. Because there are usually new doubts arising in them, counter-phobic Sixes have to go on proving they are courageous. The phobic Six, on the other hand, may try to appear harmless or funny, to avoid potential threats from the outside. The American filmmaker Woody Allen, a phobic Six, accomplished this task by making comedy out of his fear and paranoia. The goal in both the case of the phobic and counter-phobic Skeptics is to get safe. Sixes will usually manifest strong partners in the interest of safety, but they will also feel the need to continuously test the loyalty and commitment of their loved ones.

MEETING THE SKEPTIC IN US

When we lose our sense of balance concerning threats to our survival, we start to meet the Six fixation in ourselves. Our fears get overblown and out of all proportion to the reality. We start to live in a jungle world of projection, mistrust and paranoia. And we feel totally alone in this "sauve qui peut" situation where everyone is out for himself and no one cares about anyone else. Mistrust takes over our inner space and we are without access to Essence or to inner spaciousness. We become constricted, stressed out and reactive.

Experiencing the Six fixation in ourselves may also be connected to the loss of confidence, feeling deep down we don't really have what it takes to meet the challenges of life. This may mean we push ourselves, becoming hard, inflexible and rigid in our daily activity. We might experience what it means to have an "iron will". Or we may find ourselves in the grip of worry, doubt and anxiety. Pushing ourselves is usually a sign of distorted Will, or false Will. It is the way we defend against our fears of things not turning out right. In this negative frame of mind we become defensive, concerned only with holding on to what we have. We get squeezed into smaller and smaller circles of possibility, limiting our choices and our field of action.

MISTRUST

Mistrust is a kind of trance. It is a distortion of reality, a hypnotic state, a diminished field of awareness. Mistrust generates negative expectations and the tendency to create situations that bring up more mistrust in us. In our mistrust, everything becomes distorted. The rope looks like the snake. We cannot distinguish what is real from what is mistrust. If people praise us, we wonder what they really want from us. Unconsciously we expect betrayal and abandonment in our relationships. We live in mistrust, in negative expectations and distrust of others, in a trance that has its roots in our childhood.

In order to really experience Essence, we need to become aware of the distortions caused by our mistrust, otherwise there is no way to relax our defenses and protections. Mistrust contracts our inner space. In our mistrust, no one is trustworthy, no one is really there for us - and there is no way to let go, to be open or to be real. We get isolated and closed down energetically by our mistrust.

Our childhood family conditioning usually resulted in us being very political children. That means we learned to use many different survival strategies – such as fighting, pleasing, blaming, threatening, collapsing or withdrawing. We became tricky and deceitful in these strategies. As children, we started to experience ourselves as dishonest or unreliable in these strategies. We lost our sense of dignity and our confidence. We started to distrust ourselves.

Because of mistrust, we need periodic reality checks. It is important to share our mistrust. Especially for Skeptics, there's a tendency to project negative emotions onto others. These projections distort reality. We need to periodically check up on our inner reality and what we see in others. Much of what we see in others may be projection, an unconscious transfer of our own feelings onto them. Sharing our mistrust with others is the first step toward coming out of mistrust and projections.

INTEGRATING THE WHITE ESSENCE

In order to fully integrate the Will Essence we need to explore the issue of castration. We need to explore our feelings of insufficiency, incapacity and insecurity - in all forms. Castration can be described as feelings of inadequacy, feelings of "I can't". In relation to our fathers, we may have experienced a lack of support or protection, not enough guidance or emotional contact, a general lack of nurturing male presence or an absence of male energy altogether. The result is that we suffer from performance anxiety, the fear we can't make it, that we're not enough or that we can't get the job done. For men, it may be the feeling that their penis is too small, that they are weak, insignificant or helpless.

Facing our castration anxiety is part of this process of integrating the White Essence. Castration anxiety is the feeling that if we really go for what we need or want, what really supports our own development, we will be stopped or cut down in some way. Our own fathers may have been very insecure, competitive and judgmental, providing us with very little support. Or they may have been totally absent, emotionally or physically. Or our mothers may have been encouraging us to give up our will in order to get her love ("If you really love me you will do what I want you to do"). This leaves us with the feeling that if we go for what we want, if we are really our own person, we are going to get stopped or punished in some way. We may experience this as a lack of power or strength, or an absence of the capacity to express ourselves. Feelings of impotence or lack of sexual drive may also accompany these experiences. We need to confront this whole package in order to open the door to the White Essence.

The lack of inner support results in us pushing ourselves, attempting to push over our anxieties. We may go through a continual process of puffing ourselves up, then later feeling deflated. The body becomes tense and rigid in this struggle with our feelings of castration. This struggle tends to create tension in the neck, solar plexus and lower back, plus an absence of feeling in the genitals in both men and women. Therapies connected to the body are generally good for Skeptics, reawaking parts of the body that may lack energy or feeling. Bioenergetics and pulsation, for example, can be helpful, provided these techniques do not encourage more pushing.

Often we are not aware of how much our father was missing in our formative years. Somehow he was physically, emotionally or energetically absent for most of us. There was not enough father presence in our lives, not enough nurturing male presence. We need to face the pain of this deficiency, going deeply into our hunger for the father presence, for the guidance and support that was missing in our childhood. As children we yearned for the father to be there for us, to take us out of the world of mother and show us the world at large. We need to know that it is okay to be in the world. At the same time, we may also need to become aware of how much our mother made us feel guilty when we separated from her, how much conflict there is in all our separations, how much our separation fears take us out of the Will Essence.

Another aspect of integrating the White Essence is becoming aware of the superego, the way in which we castrate ourselves on the inside. By pushing and judging ourselves, often with the aggressive energy of the super ego, we lose contact with the White Essence. By blaming and condemning ourselves, we put ourselves under enormous pressure to perform, to succeed or to be perfect. We need to start to recognize this pattern in ourselves. On the inside we are creating time pressure, performance pressure and pressure to be perfect. This pressure separates us from the Will Essence.

Honestly confronting our fears of engulfment is part of integrating the Will Essence, especially for men. Fears of invasion and suffocation, fears of being overwhelmed by the significant other, often prevent men from integrating the White Essence. In some family systems the female power is all encompassing - the father only supported the mother or there was no male presence at all. Sometimes the female energy is too much for the male child and the Will Essence gets undermined. Also for men, going into the issues of the White can bring up fears or conflicts around being gay. The identification with mother may be very strong and the identification with father extremely weak. These issues need to be faced in the process of integrating the White.

A final aspect of integrating the White Essence involves getting anchored in our soul purpose. We need be in alignment with our soul mission, the purpose of our life, in order to feel solid in ourselves. This means creating a life that actualizes our soul purpose. This alignment with our spiritual purpose gives us the courage to go through the difficulties, to face the obstacles. We become aligned with our truth, we become fearless in relation to our spiritual path. We need to know what we are here for in order have this kind of inner strength. This quality is associated with Inner Commitment, a secondary quality of Essence linked to the Six. Inner Commitment releases the trauma and shock around centuries of survival fear and gives us the strength to show up, to really commit to a life of awareness and responsibility. We stop undermining ourselves. We are solid in pursuing the direction of our soul.

HEALING THE SKEPTIC

The principal difficulty of the Skeptic, whether phobic or counter-phobic, is not fear. The difficulty is all the activity that goes on around fear, all the ways Sixes try to defend against fear and the feeling they are not courageous enough. Both their inner mental activity and their outer doing is motivated by trying to get rid of fear rather than feeling it. The White Essence heals the Six because it allows them stop struggling against their fear. And when they stop struggling, the Will Essence automatically becomes more present in them.

At the heart of the Six fixation is the separation from the Daylight Essence (see Chapter 9). The line between Six and Nine on the Enneagram represents this. The Living Daylight is the quality of Universal Love, the loving light that permeates everything. It is the basic goodness of all creation. It is absolute trust. It is a quality of inner and outer safety, of love that is the fundamental nature of reality. It is our inner home. Fearlessness and dignity are its very substance. Losing contact with the Living Daylight through the shock and trauma of early childhood experiences is like the fall from grace, like paradise lost, like being expelled from the Garden of Eden.

The loss of contact with the Daylight Essence in the Skeptic results in a corresponding obsession with the Will Essence. The Skeptics are attempting to generate the White Essence, in a vain attempt to be solid, confident, courageous and grounded. Unfortunately, their adrenaline-based ego activity just produces more charged thinking, more distorted reactions, more anxiety and fear, more feelings of doubt, mistrust and suspicion. They really want to be solid and grounded and steadfast – they just can't do it. When they stop trying, healing happens. For Sixes there is often a lot of fear in their nervous system, but the primary difficulty is how much they are struggling against it. So reconnecting to the Living

Daylight can help to relax them and resolve the core panic that underlies their personality. Many Tibetan meditations are based on the Living Daylight and the White Essence. They can be effective in circulating these Essences and providing strong experiences of inner support and relaxation.

One of the ways for Sixes to heal themselves is to fall apart completely. Giving up control from the solar plexus is a way for Skeptics to really feel what is behind that control and to access the White Essence. The holding pattern in the solar plexus is like a wall that separates their lower body from their upper body. They become disconnected from the earth, from their legs, from their belly and their sex. Sometimes Sixes actually experience themselves as being above the ground rather than on it. They get disconnected from the actual physical support of their lower body. Relinquishing the control of the solar plexus breaks down this wall that separates Sixes from their guts, their sex, their life energy. Physical activity that engages both the upper and lower body can be beneficial to Sixes.

LEADERSHIP AND ORGANIZATIONS

Decision-making is not usually easy for Sixes. It tends to take time. They need to think about it. They tend to second-guess themselves and worry about decisions once they have been made. Doubt tends to undermine them in this regard. Because the Six leader gives so much importance to the downside, to what could go wrong, they can be deficient in creating a proactive vision or in seizing opportunities for their organization. Above all, Six leaders want to avoid blame. Six leaders tend to shun the spotlight and do not enjoy the public role of boss or CEO. They are excellent in crisis situations, when rallying the troops is necessary.

Six organizations frequently have something to do with information gathering, security, intelligence or law enforcement. Fire departments are usually Six organizations. Enabling others to respond to threats or crises is often the product or the service of a Six business. Internally, Six organizations are obsessed by control issues, how to prepare for emergencies. Intelligence organizations like the CIA are by their nature Six organizations. They are on the lookout for the dangerous intentions and activities of others, and they spend a lot of their time analyzing worst-case scenarios. They generate mountains of data on people and organizations, attempting to uncover intrigue and hidden agendas. They live on paranoia, on security checks and clearances. They are motivated by the desire to gain control by finding things out, especially hidden or secret things. Mistrust and suspicion are highly valued in these organizations but are often employed to undermine the authority of superiors. In their mistrust and paranoia, Six organizations can become extremely disconnected from any objective reality.

HOW TO WORK WITH SIXES

Sixes want to know where they stand with you. They know everyone has a private agenda and they need to know what your agenda is in order to feel at ease with you. They need to know your credentials, your expertise, how you know what you know. They need to know your allegiances and connections. Sixes need clear rules and guidelines, clear responsibilities in their work. They are hard workers and good at getting the job done when the task is well defined. Sixes want security and predictability in the workplace. They are traditionalists, prudent and conservative. If you present them with new ideas, make sure they know you are completely on their side, then proceed to demonstrate the value of what you propose. Sixes are looking for loyalty and safety. They need to know they can trust you, so you need to take time to build that trust and to show them you are trustworthy.

In working with Skeptics it is important to take the time to meet their doubts and concerns. That means validating their fears and misgivings, showing them that you are also concerned, then patiently demonstrating the value of what you propose. Not spending time on the negative side of a proposal can look like trying to hide something to a Six. You need to spend time on details because they want to know the details, not just the big picture. Always keep your word with Sixes. Never exaggerate. Lay things out as clearly and as straightforward as you can. Never pressure a Six – it will only create anxiety and resistance in them. Be sincere and express your trust in them.

COLLECTIVE EXPRESSIONS OF THE SKEPTIC

Germany is the archetypal collective expression of the Skeptic. Germans have an ambivalent relationship to authority that mirrors the Six Personality. They want a strong authority in their lives, but at the same time they cannot trust that authority. And in the end they always feel betrayed by that authority in some way. In the phobic mode they are more dutiful and subservient to authority, but very distrustful. In the counter-phobic mode they are rebellious, defiant and obsessed with showing how tough they are. Behind both behaviors there is fear. Hitler was a counter-phobic Six portraying himself as a reliable authority, gathering followers who idealized him. He was also portraying himself as a heroic rebel against the weakness of the Weimar Republic, against the injustices inflicted on Germany at Versailles, and so on. And the Germans bought it. And they were betrayed by their desire for a strong leader. Hitler also exhibited the classic counter-phobic Six tendency to project hostile feelings on others, and then attack them in order to feel safe.

Germany can be looked on collectively as an imitation of Will Essence. There is something very dense and solid about the German collective. All the bitchiness and grumpiness of the Germans can be seen as an attempt to be strong, solid, reliable and grounded. But this dour, sullen, obstinate way of behaving often goes more in the direction of pig-headedness and stubbornness than toward any connection to the White Essence. Germans look sturdy and solid to the max. And there is tremendous pressure in the collective to be strong, to be tough. Under their rough exterior, however, Germans are a bit mushy. They harbor a lot of doubt and insecurity. They are often fearful and in the grip of defensive reactions toward others. They are "joiners" who need to belong to groups in order to feel safe. They often feel a lack of inner support. Germans look for support on the outside in order to fill this powerful inner need. The archetype of the authoritarian German father figure, the strong leader and dominant fatherland are all part of this gestalt.

CHAPTER 7

THE HOLY FOOL
ENNEATYPE 7

Name: The Planner (Epicure, Visionary, Optimist)

Essence: Joy

Color: Yellow

Symbol: The Fool of the Tarot

Passion: Gluttony for variety

Fixation: Planning

Psychology: Narcissistic

Family Deficiency: Limited vision, narrow perspective

Ego Ideal: Global mind, the big picture, overview

Ego Confusion: Confuses Joy (Yellow Essence) with planning, excitement and frivolous activity

Mask: Always optimistic

Specific Reaction: Denial, rationalizing

Organ Affected: Small intestine

THE YELLOW ESSENCE

The Yellow Essence is a keen sense of delight, happiness, appreciation and curiosity. It is playful and innocent. The Fool of the Tarot stepping off into the abyss is its symbol. No worries. In contact with the Yellow we are blissfully ignorant. The Joy Essence is sheer amusement and playfulness. It is carefree. It is total freedom, from both the past and the future. There is a lightness of the heart in this Essence. It is spontaneous and open-hearted. Why worry? Life is just an incredible joke that most people seem to be missing.

The Yellow Essence breaks all the images, destroys all the idols, all the great ideas, all the belief systems. John Lennon's song Imagine is an anthem to this Seven longing to let go of all the systems, all the possessions, all the constraints. In the Joy Essence there is nothing to be serious about in this world, least of all the mountains of conceptual reality we live in. Joy destroys all the idols, all the holy rigmarole. Laughter is the highest form of prayer in this Essence. You make fun of the superego, you laugh at the sad seriousness of the world. In the Yellow Essence we are all diamonds shaking the dust off ourselves, we are all jewels in our own right. When we really experience the Yellow Essence, we turn away from the superego and start looking toward the light. Looking toward the source, we discover our own nature. We don't have to heal our mommy and daddy stuff, we don't need to work on ourselves anymore. We are no longer run by our deficiency, we are just living in the light. Life is a celebration.

The Yellow Essence is connected to the left side of the heart. In the Yellow we let go of all desire to improve ourselves. We let go of all the inner images of ourselves, of mother and father. We let go of all our projections. Breaking all the images means letting go of all the object relations we carry on the inside. All the internal images depart, all our identifications with them are dropped. From this place real love can happen. We appreciate others as they are.

There is curiosity and delight in discovering what is real - what is behind all the images – but it is an easy, relaxed curiosity. This Essence activates excitement, adventure and intensity. We explore the mystery of existence with joy and curiosity. There are no plans or goals to this adventure – we are just joyfully curious. Being on a spiritual path doesn't mean we have to be heavy, miserable or depressed. Our playfulness makes us fluid, flexible and creative. We laugh at our mistakes and our pretensions. We are bemused by a world that is taking itself so seriously.

THE SEVEN FIXATION

The Planner is probably the most cheerful personality type of the Enneagram. They are generally very upbeat and fun. In contact with Essence, Sevens are charming, imaginative, spontaneous and lively, bubbling with interesting projects and ideas. Out of touch with Essence, they are narcissistic, scattered, hectic, ungrounded, undisciplined, demanding and lost.

If the Observer is the introverted response to fear, then Enneatype Seven, the Planner, is the extroverted way of responding to fear. Sevens appear optimistic, enthusiastic and lighthearted, full of exciting projects and ideas, ready to taste all the exciting pleasures of life. Planning is a way to avoid the present, keeping one foot in pleasant options and future possibilities where even more pleasure will be available. They put a lot of energy into devising ever new and more exciting pleasures. Plans and backup plans are needed to avoid disappointment and to ensure a sense of freedom. Sevens are very rebellious against any constraints on their freedom. But they also have a lot of fear about how things will actually turn out and they defend against these fears by being outgoing, enthusiastic and fun. They also defend against these fears by having backup plans.

The Planner is very much in the grip of the ideal of having fun, having a good time, keeping things light, avoiding seriousness and boredom at all costs. This ideal often prevents them from facing the deeper issues in themselves. Sevens have a hard time committing themselves to anything and they tend to disappear when things get boring. Planners are fast thinkers who idealize the big picture and a broad vision of things rather than exploring all the minute details the way Fives do. Sevens search out the most interesting and ingenious ideas on a diverse range of exciting subjects. But behind the cheerful upbeat façade there is enormous stress and tension. In their guts Sevens are starving. All the buoyancy and excitement hides a deep sense of inner desolation and lifelessness. Planners generally experience intense pressure to keep up the pretense of ever-increasing pleasures and excitement. Feeling restless, hectic and unfocused on the inside, they are not really rooted in their body or their emotions, in their relationships or their work.

Sevens are permissive, self-indulgent and hedonistic. They tend to inflate their successes and minimize their defeats. Although Sevens usually appear to be confident and self-assured, their perpetual okayness hides their frustration and disappointment. They do not suffer much inner conflict but they do suffer periodic bouts of dejection and hopelessness.

Sevens lost touch with the Diamond Essence at an early age and often feel completely devoid of any Inner Guidance or direction. In this regard, they have lost touch with the natural ability to explore their inner reality, to know what is real. Often this gives them a feeling of being disoriented and lost. As children, Planners were sensitive to the narrow vision of the family and to the limited nourishment their family could provide. Often they lost the nourishing connection with mother at an early stage. They learned that they have to take care of themselves. In their relationship with mother, which was usually difficult, Planners realized they were never going to get the nourishment they desired. They made a decision to start taking care of their own needs. This meant finding friends and activities in order to prove they did not need mother. They would take care of their own needs now. The truth is that in the midst of all their interesting activities, Sevens are very needy and actually starved for real nourishment and depth. They are covering their inner emptiness and desolation with stimulating ideas and things to get excited about.

In the family of the Planner there was often a limited vision or a petty small-mindedness that Sevens experienced as poverty consciousness or an absence of freedom. They felt very stuck and marginal in this family system. And they began to idealize the big picture, a broader vision of life. This tendency sometimes goes in the direction of cosmic mind or universal mind. Sevens are very good at overview, conceptualizing things on a grand scale, synthesizing systems and ideas. The big picture is also part of keeping things interesting and exciting. Planners are so good in grasping conceptual reality that they mistake it for existential reality. Planners are often conceptually enlightened. They know everything already. And they are extremely narcissistic in the sense that they expect others to recognize and admire them for their upbeat performance, for their interesting ideas, for their exciting future plans and projects. Their narcissism is often unconscious and can be experienced by others as extremely demanding – demanding that others see them as special or superior, that others share their enthusiasm.

MEETING THE PLANNER IN OURSELVES

When we run over our real feelings in attempts to feel good or to make ourselves believe we feel good, the Seven fixation is present in us. In our desire to be interesting and optimistic, we can lose contact with our real feelings and our truth. Compensations become our crutch and frenetic behavior becomes our reality. We lose our contact with others in superficial meetings that leave us drained dry. We lose ourselves in exciting ideas and concepts. We get lost in endless future planning. Our fear prevents us from allowing a deeper connection with others, including our friends. The emphasis on feeling good, always attempting to be in one emotional mode, namely up, exhausts us and depletes our energy. By giving a positive spin to all our activities we hide our inner wasteland, our lack of inner nourishment. Our whole personality is defending against this inner dryness and deficiency. We lose touch with our connection to the body and to the full spectrum of our emotions.

SPIRITUAL NARCISSISM

Spiritual Narcissism involves seeking affirmation from others about how holy we are, how spiritual we are, how enlightened we are. This is a kind of narcissism that can be very subtle, or not so subtle. The Tibetan master Chogyam Trungpa called it "spiritual materialism". We start to make our spiritual progress into a possession that needs to be seen and applauded by others. We need to drive our spiritual accomplishments around like a teenager with a new car.

In the grip of our spiritual narcissism we want to be seen in a certain spiritual light, usually in a certain quality of Essence. We hold a static image of this Essence, of ourselves as spiritual or evolved in some way, and we get stuck in a self-image or mental construct that is divorced from Being. Our past experiences of Essence become static images that actually hinder our contact with Being. Our inner realizations become possessions. We become identified with our spiritual ideas and they just become part of our luggage, rather than a support for our liberation. We need to face the pain of our identification with spiritual self-images and religious beliefs; how much that identification separates us from Being.

Because we never got enough attention or recognition at the level of Being, we crave it. We crave being recognized in our embodiment of the different qualities of Essence. In childhood, we mainly got attention for how we looked or for our mental or physical abilities. Or we got attention for performing in other ways that pleased our parents. When someone actually acknowledges us in our Being, we are thrilled and delighted. For most of us, it is easy to become dependent on this kind of recognition, especially if the recognition comes from a mentor or a spiritual master. We get identified with the recognition, with a certain spiritual image of ourselves, and we lose contact with Being. We need to be honest about our narcissistic needs and how we satisfy those needs through our spiritual activities.

INTEGRATING THE YELLOW ESSENCE

Mother is really our heart's desire, literally our first love. But the wanting of mother gets stopped at several junctures in childhood and in adolescence. Often our wanting and desire for mother gets shut down in childhood, as does our joy and aliveness. One of the things that can support the Joy Essence is allowing ourselves to want, to desire. This is not about having - this is only about allowing ourselves to feel the desires of our heart, the desires of the child in us. Sometimes it feels risky to express desires, whether it is the desire to save the world or to eat ice cream. Because our wanting is associated with the child part of us, we judge it as not serious or not adult. Or we see the wanting of the child as unrealistic. But this is not about possessing (which quickly becomes routine), this is only about wanting. Suppressing our wanting, no matter how trivial or unrealistic the desires are, shuts down our joy. We need to allow ourselves to dream, to desire and to want – whether it is the dream of falling in love, driving a Ferrari, relaxing on a beautiful beach or eating an ice cream cone. Allowing and expressing our wanting and desire ignite the Joy Essence.

Because we are negatively merged with mother on the inside (see Chapter 2) we often hold a much stronger negative image of her than a positive one. Being joyful is usually not the emotion we connect with her. In fact, we may feel like we are betraying mother when we are joyful. This is a deep wound in the heart of the child. Guilt stops us from feeling joyful. The bonding with mother closes our heart and makes us feel as if loyalty to mom means negative merging and suffering. We need to let go of the negative merging with mother. We need to let go of the negative self-image we hold onto in order not to betray mother. Unconsciously we keep mother close to us by not being joyful. Joy feels risky and seriousness and depression feel safe. In this way we also block the endorphins in our system and prevent ourselves from experiencing the Yellow. So we need to do the work on our mother issues in order to liberate real joyousness.

Family systems are usually based on scarcity – not enough money, not enough love, not enough time, not enough something. This sense of scarcity inhibits the Joy Essence. Unconsciously we may feel that limiting ourselves is somehow the right thing to do. This may be especially true for the Perfectionist and the Observer, but it also has a truth for the other Enneatypes. Or we may feel that seriousness protects us in some way. The superego fears playfulness and aliveness, with the sad result that most adults are way too serious. We need to start to face this conditioning and to let go of it.

Because the mind loves complexity, simplicity can be a great support for our Joy. By coming out of the big picture, the global mental constructs that try to explain everything or resolve everything, we lighten up and allow the Joy Essence to live in our hearts.

Joy is also based partly on the integration of autonomy and intimacy, the relaxed interplay between these two essential aspects of our lives. Freud stated this truth by emphasizing the central role that work and love play in our psychological wellbeing. If we cannot fully live both of these dimensions of life, we cannot really be joyful. In terms of Essence, the integration of intimacy and autonomy is most clearly associated with the Pearl Essence. As we master the healthy interplay between intimacy and autonomy, we can begin to enjoy the dance of aloneness and togetherness. Trying to live only on one side of this duality creates a lot of unhappiness. When one is favored over the other, we experience conflict, drama and anxiety in the movement between these two vital areas of our life. With the integration of intimacy and autonomy in our lives, we can start to move between these two dimensions with more ease and relaxation. We can begin to experience this movement with anticipation and Joy.

Letting go of the loved ones is also part of nurturing the Yellow Essence in us. As we continue to let go of the images of the loved ones that we hold inside, the Joy Essence emerges. As we let go of our self-images, especially self-images linked to the beloved ones, we create more inner freedom and Joy. This does not mean that we are not caring or loving. Real caring and love are a natural expression of our Joy. When we realize that the world doesn't need more suffering, we can begin to value our Joy. When we realize that guilt and depression are just old ways to pull ourselves down, we can dance this life joyfully.

HEALING THE PLANNER

The healing direction for the Seven is first allowing themselves to connect with how much sadness and pain there is under the happy exterior, how much stress and tension their involvement in false personality is causing them. The Planner personality is basically an imitation of the Yellow Essence - a disconnection from the real qualities of delight, appreciation, curiosity, playfulness and innocence. Instead of a lightness of heart and a carefree attitude toward life, Sevens are actually in deep denial of their real feelings. When Planners realize it is not really Joy they are creating in their lives, then they can relax some of their activity around always being optimistic and cheerful. When they can give themselves the permission to feel their deeper feelings, their sadness and heartache, for example, real healing can begin.

When Planners realize how obsessive they are around pleasure and anticipating pleasure, real celebration can begin. When they realize how much frustration and anxiety they experience by living in anticipation, in pleasant future possibilities, they can begin the journey back to being present in all the dimensions of now. The gluttony of the Seven is to taste everything and to do everything. It is this gluttony for variety that covers a deeper sense of being starved for nourishment. Planners need to reconnect with their experience of inner nourishment. Part of this healing means risking to experience the full range of their feelings, including the unpleasant ones.

At the same time, Sevens need to experience the truth that planning is not guidance. They need to begin to reconnect with the true Inner Guidance, the Diamond Essence. The line between Seven and Five represents this disconnection from guidance in childhood. Because Planners are so good in understanding and organizing conceptual reality, they easily get lost in their global visions of how things are. These global mental constructs leave Planners disoriented and lost because they are not connected to their gut feelings or their real needs. Sevens tend to hold onto static concepts of how their inner process should develop. The Diamond Essence can bring Sevens back to the truth of the here and now, to direct inquiry into their personal reality rather than depending on concepts and ideas. Sevens need to back off their goal-oriented preoccupation with the future and find their way back to the present moment, the only place where Inner Guidance can be found.

Patience is a virtue, especially for Sevens. In the rush to experience the variety of life, Sevens put themselves under pressure to keep moving in a way that limits their ability to integrate Essence, not just the Joy Essence. Because of past difficulties with a particular Essence, often associated with shock or trauma, we sometimes bury or disown a particular quality of Essence. This may result in a phobic dislike for a particular color or an activity associated with that Essence. Patience gives us the needed time it takes to integrate Essence and heal past wounds. Sevens are especially in need of the time and patience it takes for this healing process to take place.

LEADERSHIP AND ORGANIZATIONS

Sevens enjoy brainstorming and innovative thinking more than they like to actually make decisions. They tend not to see decisions as final but rather as a step along the road to a greater vision. They want decisions to enhance future options, not limit them. In their visionary zeal, Seven leaders can be lacking in patience, realism and follow-through. Planners dislike hierarchies, routine and activity they consider boring. They often manage by decentralizing power and by creating a certain amount of chaos around them.

"Thriving on Chaos" by Tom Peters is a Seven manifesto. Sevens are egalitarians that allow a lot of freedom in their style of leadership. They encourage an atmosphere where the creative exchange of ideas flourishes. Traditional command and control management is usually not their style.

Seven organizations are allergic to hierarchy. Teams tend to be loose associations of professionals who need little supervision. At their best, Seven organizations can be very innovative and imaginative in the way they conduct business. They are often hotbeds of creativity. Seven organizations tend to function well in situations that need a lot of flexibility and innovation to survive. Individuality and experimentation are hallmarks of the Seven organization. Supervision and control are not. These organizations are usually great when it comes to changing directions at a moment's notice or to responding creatively to market changes.

HOW TO WORK WITH SEVENS

To get along with Sevens you need to match their upbeat energy and enthusiasm. Let them enjoy their excitement in creative ideas and concepts. Allow yourself to be optimistic around them, without dwelling on the down side or the worst-case scenario. Planners want to think about exciting possibilities – not about what can't be done or what could go wrong. Give them plenty of space and plenty of choices. Trying to limit them in some way will make for aggressive reactions. Make your presentations exciting, emphasizing the big picture and not getting bogged down in details. Ask them a lot of questions. They love to talk and to hear themselves express their vision. They are quick thinkers who can synthesize diverse systems and concepts fast. Rules, hierarchies, routine and control will put them off. Sevens, however, need firm boundaries and deadlines because it is easy for them to lose the distinction between fantasy and reality.

COLLECTIVE EXPRESSIONS OF THE PLANNER

All the countries of South America have something to do with the Planner fixation. And most of these countries are squarely in the Seven fixation. Brazil and Venezuela represent two typically Seven countries. Planning tends to mean no firm plans, which means keeping all options open in order to defend against the risk of possible boredom. No one is ever on time, except by accident, and there are always several backup plans. Being an hour or two late for an appointment is not a problem. When Venezuelan business-men go to New York for the first time they often miss appointments because they cannot understand that nine o'clock actually means nine o'clock to the North Americans.

There is an atmosphere of celebration and festivity in the collective atmosphere of Seven countries. The atmosphere is buoyant and upbeat. People like to party and to keep things light. People are laid back, the music is great and the food is good. It is a perpetual carnival that operates in almost total denial of its dark side. The dark side is that poverty and violence are endemic, the distribution of wealth is terribly lopsided, there is an absence of economic and social mobility and government policy is often destructive to the social and economic fabric of the society. The Seven fixation is a way of surviving through denial. "It's not so bad" is the Seven refrain.

CHAPTER 8

FIRE IN THE BELLY
ENNEATYPE EIGHT

Name: The Boss (Leader, Chief)

Essence: Strength

Color: Red

Symbol: Fire

Passion: Lust for life

Fixation: Vengeance

Psychology: Sociopath

Family Deficiency: Conflicts or confusion around power

Ego Ideal: Justice, fairness

Ego Confusion: Confuses Strength (Red Essence) with anger, aggression and control

Mask: Always strong

Specific Reaction: Get revenge

Organs Affected: Pituitary gland, liver, perineum

THE RED ESSENCE

The Red Essence is vitality and strength, passion and intensity. The Strength Essence gives us physical, spiritual, mental and emotional strength – it charges and energizes our whole system. The Red

Essence is fire, passion for life. The Red Essence is the energy that wakes us up. It is the energy we need in order to stand on our own two feet, to stand up for ourselves, to be our own person. It supports our aliveness, our yes to life, our courage to dive into life with all our energy. The Strength Essence is about activation, actualization and expansion. It gives us the courage to take risks, to accept the challenges of life, the courage to act and to take responsibility for our actions. The Red Essence turns us on to life in all its dimensions.

The Strength Essence is connected to the right side of the body, the liver and the right side of the heart. The right side represents our active self, our doing side, our participation in life. It is a very male quality of Essence, outgoing and expressive, as well as being one of the most dynamic and personal qualities of Essence. It is eminently human. It gives us the courage to be human in the midst of humanity. The Red Essence informs us very directly that we are not on this planet to be monks or recluses – we are here to participate fully in life. We are here to seek the truth of our humanness, to live our truth in the marketplace.

In the famous Zen parable of the taming the bull, the spiritual seeker starts by chasing the bull, then catching it by the tail, and finally subduing the bull and leading it homeward. But that is not the end of the story. Yes, that may be enlightenment for some - finally subduing the delusions of the mind - but it is not the end of the parable. Once the bull is tethered, the enlightened man heads off with an empty wine bottle in his hand, going to the market to have the bottle filled and to participate in ordinary life. Enlightenment in this case means full participation in ordinary life. It means becoming more and more human. Red wine is also a symbol of the Red Essence.

The Red Essence gives us the courage to separate, on the inside, from the world of our parents. It is a feeling of standing up on the inside - respecting ourselves, valuing ourselves and standing up for ourselves. We no longer live in reaction to others. We can express our truth without pushing others away. The Red Essence is one of the key supports for our individuation, our autonomy and our spiritual maturity. In touch with the Strength Essence, we can risk being the unique human being that we in fact are. Freedom and independence are intrinsic qualities of the Red.

The Red Essence also gives us the courage to face our childhood wounds, to face our inner demons, to face the beast inside of us. This means facing the part of us that is pure hatred and doesn't want love or anything else, except destruction. The Red Essence gives us the courage to face our cowardice, to face the fact that we could not stand up to mother and father in childhood, the fact that we were humiliated, shamed or broken by the family system. This means facing our violence, in all its forms - emotional, mental and physical. This means becoming aware of our abusive and controlling behaviors. There can be no real peace inside of us until we have faced this part of us and made our peace with it.

The Red Essence is the feeling of fire in the belly. This fire is connected to the perineum and the genitals. It is like a fire burning in the base chakras or energy centers. It is the energy of becoming - life happening in all its chaos and intensity moment to moment. The Red Essence generates tremendous heat in us, rising from the base of the spine. It is Shakti energy. It is ecstatic passionate love. The Red Essence tells us to wake up and roar like a lion. The Strength Essence wakes us up to our desires and our needs - to our yes for life. The Red Essence is the fiery energy of anger without the activity of anger. It is anger that turns us on. It is an old rock song blasting "C'mon baby light my fire". But in the case of the Red Essence you light your own fire. The Red provides us with the stamina and perseverance to confront and conquer the difficulties of life. It provides us with the desire to dive into life with a sense of divine madness – like a wild man or wild woman. With the Red Essence present in us, we delight in the challenges of life.

THE BOSS FIXATION

Bosses are the tough guys of the Enneagram. They have a lot of intensity and force of character that is usually easy to recognize. In contact with the Red Essence, Eights are direct, authoritative, self-confident, loyal, earthy, dynamic and independent. Separated from the Red Essence they can be aggressive, bullying, ruthless, destructive and revengeful.

Along with the Perfectionist and the Peacemaker, Enneatype Eight is part of the control types, the anger types. Their bodies tend to be very sturdy and solid, heavily armored and insensitive to pain. Bosses are thick-skinned, physically and emotionally. The core belief is "I have to be strong, otherwise I won't survive." Being strong and staying in control is a life or death issue for Boss types. They are ready for conflict and willing to escalate - and they know they are going to win, because they have to. Eights love confrontation because it revs them up, activates their anger and gives them energy. Anger makes them feel strong. They hold their ground, they never give up - and they dominate the playing field of their life.

When you see the Boss type in a crowded room, they stand out with an intensity and strength of presence that marks them out as not just one of the crowd. Eights have tremendous passion to consume life. They come on strong, in everything. They are often burning the candle at both ends. They are very dynamic and energetic people. Eights are consuming life at such a furious pace it is sometimes hard for others to keep up with them. They have enormous energy to get things done, to surmount obstacles and to get what they want in the end.

In the childhood of Eights there was not enough freedom to explore. Boss types were over controlled or held responsible for things they could not control. They felt unfairly blamed and humiliated. This gives Bosses a tremendous reservoir of anger and rage, a perpetual sense of injustice that is like an active volcano bubbling inside. They were forced to be adults before they really got a chance be children. For adult Eights, the issue is control of a hostile environment that they have to dominate in order to survive. They need to defend themselves in order to avoid being run over the way they were in childhood.

Anger is the engine that drives the Boss. The simmering volcano of anger inside them can explode at any minute. And there is very little time between what triggers their anger and the anger response itself. The anger and rage of the Eight is a desire for truth and justice. And their anger cuts through a lot of bullshit and tells the Eight who is who, what is what. They need to fight you in order to trust you. The anger is also a desire for real independence, separation from the land of parents, the land of childhood. It is a desire for individuation and autonomy. Eights are fiercely independent and often feel they have to do everything by themselves. The problem with the anger of the Eight is that it is often out of control and can alienate others, especially loved ones. When they are at the mercy of their rage and anger, dumping their fierce loathing and resentment on others, Eights are completely in the grip of their fixation. They are getting revenge for past injustices. They are settling scores.

The actual source of their rage is in the humiliation and abuse of early childhood. Eights are raging against the injustices of a childhood that they are often no longer in touch with. They have denied their childhood wounds in a very thorough way, often through the idealization of an abusive parent. Not really in contact with the source of their rage, they are just raging at whatever or whoever is not responding to their desire for domination and control. As children, Eights felt they were too sweet, too weak. "No one is ever going to run over me again" became their personal code. They defend themselves by attacking. They go for what they want and they get high on anger. The expression of anger and rage makes them feel alive and powerful. It is anger addiction. It revs them up. Eights have found their drug and it is anger. As they were abused in childhood, so they tend to abuse others in adulthood. Often they are angry with people who have little to do with the source of their fears of losing control or their sense of injustice.

MEETING THE BOSS IN US

When we are in positions of authority, we tend to meet the Boss fixation in us. We may feel we have to defend our position of authority. Or we may feel the need to control others in order to guarantee outcomes. If we are responsible for the success of a business, this may bring up our combative side and the fear of losing control. All these things will push us toward the Boss fixation. We may feel that we are indispensable, that others cannot get the job done without us. And we may start to experience a lot of anger when things don't go right. We may experience the power of our anger to control others.

When we seek revenge, we also meet the Boss inside. We may find ourselves nursing our sense of betrayal or injustice and start looking for ways to get revenge, to settle scores. The old adage "Don't get mad get even" could be updated for Boss types to read: "Get mad and get even." When we harbor a grudge for many years, like villagers who refuse to speak to each other for decades because of some misunderstanding, we are in the Boss fixation.

THE INNER CRITIC

We face our superego, our inner critic, at every stage of the spiritual journey. Our critical self usually stands in the way of our experience of essential qualities. In the superego there is both a commanding self and a critical self. There is one part that is pushing us, telling us to do more, and there is another part that is criticizing, telling us we didn't do it right. Often these internalized voices of authority figures are like the voice of God inside of us - all-powerful and always right. With its pushing and judging, this inner critic can disconnect us from our adult resources, from the different qualities of Essence.

We need to become much more familiar with our inner critic in order for it to become a healthy part of our ego structure. We need to begin to recognize the energy of the superego, where the voices come from, what kinds of situations trigger them, which persons in our life they are connected to and so on. Our personality type also determines what type of superego we have. Depending on our fixation, our critical self will push us or judge us in a particular way. For example, the superego of the Boss will push them to be stronger, whereas the superego of the Performer will push them to do more.

When we feel under attack from the inner critic, we need to defend ourselves. This may be something as simple as realizing how old and mechanical the criticism is and getting fed up with it. Enough! Or it may mean bringing a sense of humor to the inner critic. Having a good laugh can relax our connection to the superego. Because there is usually some element of truth in the judgments of our superego, we need to be able to separate what is true from the aggressive energy of the inner critic, saying yes to the truth and no to the aggression.

INTEGRATING THE RED ESSENCE

Experiencing anger is crucial to integrating the Red Essence. Anger supports our aliveness and our life energy. Often we are holding judgments about our anger, our sexuality or our aliveness that prevent us from really experiencing the Strength Essence. Sleepiness and depression are often signs of repressed anger. Disowned anger takes the form of projecting anger onto others, attracting angry people into our lives or making others feel guilty about their anger. These are all signs that the Red Essence has not been integrated. For example, we provoke others in order to get contact with their Red Essence, instead of living it ourselves.

As with the Gold Essence, the fear of really separating from mother can also stop us from living the Red Essence. Mother represents the Gold Essence. We are merged with her positive states, her love and caring; and we are merged with her negative states, her agitation and anxiety. She is who we are on many levels. So the process of separating from her is usually a long one. Part of what stops our healthy separation from mother is our fear of losing the Gold Essence, losing the sweetness or the sense of belonging. The Gold is such a yummy quality, so delicious and nourishing, we fear giving it up when we separate from mother. Fear of losing the Gold Essence often stops us from living the Red. We need to face our fears of being excluded, being judged or rejected, when we really start living our Strength.

We may literally "see red" a lot as we come closer to integrating the Red Essence. We may find ourselves wearing red clothes more often, or we may find the color red coming into our lives in other ways. We may also find that our level of energy and aliveness has increased, that we can actually enjoy our anger, that we can harness the energy of anger creatively. This may involve finding ways to vent our anger that feel both safe and satisfying. As we start to really grow up in the integration of the Red Essence, we leave for good the world of our parents. The integration of the Red Essence is a key to mature adulthood, giving us the courage and stamina to live and thrive in the marketplace.

HEALING THE BOSS

As with the other personality types, the first step to healing for

Eights is recognizing that their personality is an imitation of Essence. It is the recognition at all levels – physical, emotional, mental – that the strength they have been living and expressing is based on false personality, false Red Essence. It is the recognition that their desire for justice is part of their mask, part of their difficulty with expressing anger in a healthy way. When Bosses realize that they are in fact strong and they don't have to prove it anymore, the healing can begin. This healing involves the recognition that they no longer need to go through life like bulldozers. When the intensity of the Boss type is no longer based on the fear of losing control, they can begin to be the dynamic leaders and mentors they were meant to be. When Eights begin to see that real strength is having the courage to face their own demons, the healing has begun.

When Eights stop confusing the Red Essence with anger, aggression and control – their whole personality starts to relax and unwind, releasing many qualities of Essence. It is a healing process that releases them from their fixation and allows them to live in the light of Essence, the light of who they really are. They can relax. The war is over.

Another key to healing the Boss is healing their relationship to anger. The Red Essence is about being an adult - taking full responsibility for all our acts, including the ways we express anger. In order to fully integrate the Red Essence, Boss types need to begin to find healthy expressions of anger. They need to start to work with their anger in order to understand it and manage it in a healthier way. We all need the energy of anger to stand up for ourselves, to face the challenges of life, to set limits (say no to what is not okay). But the anger of false personality is hurtful, causing harm to our relations with friends and love ones. Eights need to honestly face their difficulties with anger and begin their own anger management program. A first step can involve becoming aware of the fact that there is very little gap between what triggers their anger and the expression of anger. Gradually increasing this gap between what triggers anger and the actual expression of anger can help Eights to bring more awareness to their anger.

Another step in the healing process for Eights is becoming aware of their disconnection from the Gold Essence. Merging Love helps to discharge the nervous system. The Gold Essence lubricates the nervous system and allows us to relax and let go. It is soothing to the nervous system. Eights are constantly charging the nervous system with their anger, without having any way to discharge it. They are missing the Gold Essence, which lubricates and soothes the nervous system. This often puts them in the ready-to-explode mode. The result is that Eights dump their anger on others just to discharge the nervous system. Violent expressions of anger are sometimes the only way for Eights to release the pressure.

At the core of the Boss is the sweetness of Gold Essence. Eights are like a tank with a Teddy bear inside. As children, the Boss types were very much in touch with their sweetness. But this sweetness could not really be supported by the family system. Eights made a decision at some point to turn their backs on the sweetness of the Gold Essence in order to be strong. Now they need to reconnect with the Gold Essence, facing the childhood wounds connected to its loss. Again Eights need to understand that real strength means facing these wounds. Eights need to know it is okay to be receptive and soft, without confusing that receptivity with weakness.

The line between Eight and Two on the Enneagram actually represents two disowned Essences related to the Boss – the Gold Essence and the Chandelier, which is Pleasure. Eights have gotten disconnected from their ability to experience pleasure. Although Eights live their appetites intensely and often overdo everything, real pleasure seems to elude them. Although they usually manifest a lot in material terms, Eights often derive comparatively little pleasure from their accomplishments. Bosses need to begin to enjoy themselves more. They need to stop taking life so seriously.

LEADERSHIP AND ORGANIZATIONS

Bosses are take-charge autocratic leaders who call the shots and don't fear taking responsibility for their decisions. Eights enjoy exercising power. They thrive on difficult situations, struggle and conflict. Eight leaders are ready to use their power to crush those who don't measure up to their code of justice, toughness and truth. They are dynamic powerhouses who motivate others with their bravado and brash intensity. At the same time, they can also be domineering and intimidating to their employees. "My way or the highway" pretty much expresses this style of authority. "You are either with me or against me, there can be no middle ground."

The Eight organization represents a classical managerial style where a hard-driving, highly motivated leader sets the pace and everyone else follows - or leaves. The Eight organization functions by decree rather than consensus. This style of organization normally does well in unstable business environments and in highly competitive markets. The Eight organization is at its best when empires are being built and daring entrepreneurship is required. Eight businesses are good in hanging tough against the competition, the government and anyone else they have to stand up to. Sooner or later they grind down the competition or gobble them up. Microsoft is the archetypal Eight organization.

WORKING WITH EIGHTS

Many Eights have difficulty working for others. They usually need to be their own boss or they need to have a section of the organization that they control. Otherwise, they tend to undermine the power structure. Some Eights can also work well in an Eight organization, provided the rules of the power game are clear to them or they can identify with the power structure. In order to get along with Eights, you need to be straight with them and match their intensity. Beating around the bush or delving into subtleties won't work. Challenging their authority or telling them what they can't do will cause "hot" reactions in them. They need to feel they are in charge and in control. Never try to con them or bullshit your way around them. It won't work. You need to be able to tolerate their outbursts of anger without confronting them directly. If you confront them directly they will go ballistic. Stand your ground, acknowledging their strength and your own.

COLLECTIVE EXPRESSIONS OF THE BOSS

As a collective expression of the Boss type, Israel is a good example. For Israel, the Holocaust represents the horror of being run over in the past, in childhood. The country being surrounded by enemies gives Israel a very real hostile environment they have to control and dominate in order to survive. Israelis are a very passionate and dynamic people with a tremendous appetite for life. They are often loud and brazen. In conflict situations they are in your face and ready to escalate. The Israeli leader Ariel Sharon, a classic Boss type, was nicknamed "the bulldozer." He resonated deeply with the Israeli collective and was one of the most trusted leaders Israel ever had. Under the rough exterior Israelis can be very sweet. At the same time, they can never let down their guard, they always have to be ready to defend themselves - or risk annihilation. Defending oneself is a life-or-death issue. Feelings of vulnerability are not well tolerated. A lot of energy goes into protection, and the best way to protect is to attack, as the state of Israel has done repeatedly in its short history. And Israel's control over the Palestinians is abusive and destructive, a violation of basic human rights, including the right to life.

There are many other Eight countries, including Spain, Mexico, Greece, Turkey, Serbia and Algeria. These are countries of high intensity and strict codes of behavior. The films of the Serbian filmmaker Emir Kusturica often portray this passionate, violent world of the Eight fixation. Eight countries usually have in their history colonization and empire, control over other countries or peoples. More often than not there is also civil war in their history or some kind of ethnic strife. Life is a battleground. Greece, for example, had a hard time preparing to host the Olympics because everyone in Greece wants to be the boss. Greeks fight each other and undermine each other a lot. The bullfight is a quintessentially Eight ritual that ends with the very real death of the adversary.

Another excellent example of the collective expression of the Boss personality is the Mafia. Out of the good intention to defend the people of Sicily from foreign control and injustice, the Mafia was born. It generated tremendous loyalty and gratefulness among the people and gave them a sense of control over their own destiny. And like the Eight fixation, born of the good intention not to be run over by others, the Mafia gradually became an abusive, punishing scourge of Sicilian society. Revenge and vendetta became a way of life.

CHAPTER 9

GRACE

ENNEATYPE 9

Name: The Peacemaker (Mediator, Negotiator)

Essence: Universal Love (basic goodness)

Color: Daylight/Living Daylight

Symbol: The Kingdom of Shambhala

Passion: Inner laziness

Fixation: Indolence

Psychology: Passive-aggressive

Family Deficiency: Absence of harmony, peace

Ego Ideal: Ordinariness

Ego Confusion: Confuses Universal Love (Daylight Essence) with harmonizing relations with others

Mask: Always calm

Specific Reaction: Space out, disconnect

Organ Affected: Pineal gland

THE DAYLIGHT ESSENCE

The Daylight Essence is the natural order of existence, the natural goodness of existence. The sun is here to provide warmth, the water to quench thirst, the air to breathe and the trees to give shade.

Existence is a benediction. We may experience it as ecstatic or blissful, or as ordinary and simple, but it is pure goodness. Universal love is a state of grace, boundless grace.

The Living Daylight is the basic goodness of existence. The nature of existence is love. Universal Love means that the whole universe is bathed in loving light. It is an all-inclusive goodness. Of the many different qualities of love (in Sanskrit there are more than 100 words for love) the Living Daylight is the highest form of love. It is boundless presence, the absence of limits or boundaries. Universal Love is the Absolute manifesting through the heart. It is intimately connected to the breath – we literally breathe in love. And we disappear in that love, in the breath of each moment, in an ecstatic vulnerability and receptivity of the heart.

In Tibetan Buddhism, the Daylight Essence is called Bodhicitta or Awakened Heart. In this quality of Essence we experience the heart as naked, exposed and vulnerable. An insect lands on your arm and you are deeply touched. This quality contains the sadness and the tenderness of the empty heart, the heart as empty space. There is a sweet soreness in the heart, a heightened sensitivity that is touched by everything. In this experience of Universal Love, the more you share the more you have to share. There is no limit to it. We are just so touched by the whole of existence, by the miracle of existence. Universal Love is one of the most beautiful qualities of Essence, a combination of bliss, tenderness and longing. Universal Love puts us in contact with the whole of existence, in a deep intimacy with all sentient beings and with every atom of existence. In this quality we feel we are living on air, nourished by each ecstatic breath.

For Tibetan Buddhists the Living Daylight is often associated with the mythical Kingdom of Shambhala, a spiritual ideal that includes the spiritual warrior. The dignity of the warrior, the fearlessness of the Samurai, is inherent in the Living Daylight. This does not mean that we do not experience fear in this dimension, only that there is no fighting with fear or dealing with fear. Fear doesn't stop us from doing what needs to be done. The concept of death doesn't really enter this dimension of love. The Living Daylight is total surrender to the boundless dimension of existence. It is total trust and supreme dignity. The Living Daylight is both the openness and the vulnerability of a sleeping baby, and the fearlessness of the spiritual warrior. This quality has an inner sense of discipline and morality that is a law unto itself. It is not strict or righteous, it is more like an uprightness, a quality of that does not slouch, collapse or contract in any way. The Daylight Essence is simplicity, directness and courage. It is the sacred path of the warrior.

Universal Love is home. In psychology, it is the ideal holding environment. It is a sense of inner and outer safety. The whole of existence is love and the body feels like loving light. This absolute sense of safety fosters a loving kindness, an availability and generosity of heart. St. Francis embodies the Living Daylight when he attracts the birds and the animals. They feel the safety and the gentleness of this love. Absolute trust.

THE NINE FIXATION

In touch with Essence, Nines are peaceful, generous, patient, receptive, supportive and empathic. They make great mediators who know how to smooth out differences between others.

Disconnected from Essence they can be sleepy, passive, procrastinating, spaced out and boring. Peacemakers tend to fall asleep on the inside. Habit and routine are their allies in this sleepwalking. They love to cruise in mechanical behaviors without really being connected on the inside.

For the Peacemaker, anger is a dangerous energy and they go numb rather than feel it. They space out a lot or go on automatic – anything to avoid feelings of anger and rage. Nines feel that if they really let their anger out they will destroy everything. In childhood, they felt any expression of anger toward mother would bring down their whole world. One of their greatest fears is being separated from loved ones. They rarely initiate separation in intimate relationships. Their disconnection from anger means they often feel resigned and disconnected from their life energy. It is safer for Nines to feel sadness than to feel the rage that lies beneath the sadness. So Peacemakers go unconscious around anger, space out, disconnect. Nines are at the center of the anger types, but they have great difficulty experiencing anger. This numbing process makes Nines passive and sleepy, or lazy and dull. There is a fundamental lack of intensity in the Peacemaker and it is coupled with a strong desire to harmonize relations with others.

As children, Nines felt overlooked, feeling that other people's needs and desires were more important than their own. They became complacent and agreeable, submitting to the priorities of others. Usually overshadowed by siblings, they knew they were not going to be seen or heard. They seem to have renounced their narcissistic needs at an early stage, contenting themselves with small comforts, easy routine and substitutes for love. They fall asleep to their own needs and desires. Peacemakers tend to go along with other people's agendas in order to keep their connection to others. And other people's wishes always seem more pressing, more urgent than their own.

The Nine style of behavior is passive-aggressive. Peacemakers avoid confrontation by accommodating others. They say yes to everyone, while often being forgetful or negligent about their commitments. They express their anger in many small ways, often unconsciously. Saying yes is part of making everyone else feel okay, for the sake of avoiding conflict with others. Nines are driven by a strong desire not to rock the boat. It's a mellow cruising in the ocean of okayness. The truth is that in their need for psychological comfort, Nines have totally lost touch with themselves.

There is a loss of the capacity for inner exploration in the Nine coupled with an aversion for psychological understanding. The inner world of the Nine has been abandoned in some way. From the outside, Peacemakers look easygoing, good natured, earthy and comfortable. But this outer calm has been accomplished through the disconnection from their inner world, the abandoning of their core needs and desires. They are actually very resigned and very stoic.

Peacemakers idealize ordinariness, confusing it with the Living Daylight. They present an unassuming, unpretentious picture. Nines don't want to shine or stand out from the crowd. They value plainness and simplicity. Hence they are often in the background, in secondary roles or support positions, giving attention to others. They have abnegated their need to be the center of attention or to receive recognition and praise. This denial of their narcissistic needs can manifest unconsciously as a ruthless desire to succeed, in violent explosions of anger, or in other ways. Real priorities tend to get forgotten by Nines. Forgetting is a way of diverting attention from what they really want in life. They easily get lost in addictive habits like watching TV or taking alcohol. They always seem to be procrastinating because they literally forget their real priorities in trivial pursuits or in diversions. Important decisions tend to get put off indefinitely and there is always plenty of time, always tomorrow. Nines usually feel there is lot to be done, but they easily lose track of what is actually important. There is a loss if inner direction and purpose in Nines.

MEETING THE PEACEMAKER IN OURSELVES

When we narcotize ourselves with television, drugs, alcohol or food we start to enter into the land of the Nine Fixation. When we deny our anger or stuff it down, we lose contact with our life energy. This deadening process, which is strongly connected to the Nine fixation, feels safe but is actually dangerous for our relationships and our personal wellbeing. When we lose touch with our passion and our true feelings, we start to enter the Nine fixation. We start to go unconscious in a way that separates us from others and from our true needs. It is as if we just want to get through life in some kind of drowsy activity that doesn't hurt too much but doesn't really feel good either. When we lose ourselves in habitual patterns, we get separated from our aliveness, creativity and imagination. We get lost in the deep Peacemaker sleep of forever being understanding, patient, diplomatic and calm.

SHOCK AND TRAUMA

Shock and trauma are the result of events that breach the protection of the holding environment. These are usually events that we can't handle, where we feel powerless, helpless or overwhelmed. Usually trauma and shock events are connected to the loss of boundaries, safety or control. Shock and trauma responses are provoked by violence or the threat of violence, by sexual or emotional abuse, by pressure and expectations, by sudden losses or separations, by abandonment or deprivation. Our nervous system is overwhelmed. It responds by becoming over-activated (as in trauma) or by going numb (as in shock). In the trauma response, we may be hyperactive, hyper-vigilant, unable to relax. In the shock response we may be spaced out, sleepy, dull, cut off.

We need to recognize shock and trauma and the events, large or small, which cause shock or trauma in us. We need to validate our response and understand it as a normal response of the nervous system. Since there is often a lot of shame around shock and trauma, we also need to share the event with others in order to come out of that shame. We need to have compassion for ourselves when we experience shock or trauma. If past trauma is causing us chronic difficulties, we need to seek professional help.

Because the nervous system cannot respond normally, shock or trauma cannot be completely discharged from the nervous system. In that way shocks and traumas are stored in the body as a contraction, a frozen place, a place where energy is blocked or doesn't flow easily. The work with Essence can help to unblock these areas of contraction.

Shock and trauma are connected to the issue of boundaries and setting limits. We need firm yet flexible boundaries. We need to have clear physical and emotional boundaries. When someone doesn't respect our personal space it is an invasion of our boundaries. Or when someone tells us what we should be feeling or gives us unwanted advice, it is a violation of our boundaries. We need to be clear about our need for boundaries and set healthy limits.

INTEGRATING THE DAYLIGHT ESSENCE

In order to integrate the Daylight Essence we need to begin to focus on the lack of holding in our childhood environment. The lack of physical or emotional support may have damaged our sense of security. The lack of nurturing support in our childhood may have had a big role in our growing up. Shock and trauma may have been regular events in our childhood, creating mistrust, anxiety and fear. The Living Daylight is our sense of home. When our sense of home gets broken, our trust gets broken too. When the goodness of God or the goodness of existence gets destroyed in the child, it is usually a big shock. We need to explore our mistrust and begin to become aware of just how much mistrust there is in our lives, in our relationships, in our daily lives.

Basic trust also has a structure issue in it. If there was some structure in our original family – if both parents were physically present in the home, for example - it usually creates a greater sense of safety for the child. When one or both parents are absent, or when there is unpredictability or threat of violence in the family system, then there is a lack of safety for the child. This is where the issues related to shock and trauma start to develop. The lack of an inner sense of safety prevents us from surrendering to the Living Daylight – it is too dangerous. So we need to begin to look at the safety issue in our childhood and work with it in order to integrate the Living Daylight. The presence of safety in childhood gives children a more resilient psychological structure. Trauma can impair normal development and normal functioning. And safety is also necessary in order for us to have a stable adult life. We need safety to expand and to grow. We also need safety to heal, so that the shock and trauma held in the nervous system can release. Without safety, the perineum and the solar plexus contract in rock-like hardness and there is no way to relax our protections.

Unfortunately we live on a scary planet, especially scary for children. The child part of us resonates with this scariness. Global warming, rising sea levels and the destruction of entire ecosystems are now part of our reality. Starvation, Aids, wars, earthquakes and poverty – all put children more at risk than adults. The abuse and exploitation of children is rampant in many parts of our world. Family structure is often broken, damaged or weak. What children are experiencing in increasingly large numbers is the absence of safety, the absence of a secure holding environment. And we are all affected by this absence of safety on our planet. We need to be consciously aware of this lack of safety in the collective and how it affects us.

For many of us, our inner psychological dynamic may feel unsafe. Severe superego attacks, for example, or patterns of cutting off on the inside may make us feel unsafe. Or we may experience emotional activity that feels unsafe, such as raging anger or fears of losing emotional control. Or our thought processes may feel unsafe, as in thoughts of suicide. So we may also need to examine the safety of our inner world in order to integrate the Living Daylight.

Retreats in natural surroundings or time spent in spiritual communities can support our experience of the Living Daylight. The contact with others who share similar concerns, values and aspirations can help to put us in touch with Universal Love. Giving ourselves the luxury of these communal experiences can be an important way to experience and integrate the Living Daylight.

HEALING THE PEACEMAKER

As with the other personality types, the first step in healing is realizing that their fixation is an imitation of Essence. When Nines begin to realize that their pleasant, accommodating, easygoing disposition is not the Living Daylight, then they can start to relax their fixation. For example, they can begin to realize that relationships also need conflict, disagreements and honesty in order to advance. Nines need to know that love can also mean not being diplomatic and patient but being straight. Relaxing their fixation can begin to give them more contact with Being, especially with the quality of Universal Love. More experiences of Universal Love will help them re-establish a healthy connection to their inner world. It will start to wake them up to the wonder and the mystery of life.

Nines need to begin to know that anger has two dimensions, a destructive one and a healing, energizing one. As part of the healthy direction, they need to start expressing their anger directly to the people they are unhappy with instead of kicking the dog when they are actually angry with the boss or a co-worker. Because there is usually a long gap between their anger and the recognition they are angry, Nines need to start to become more aware of their anger. They need to know that anger can be expressed in ways that deepen relationships rather than destroying them. They need to actually practice getting angry and having their anger validated in some way. Perhaps they need to establish some ground rules with their intimate partner so that they can express anger toward their partner in a way that feels safe. Realizing that conflict is a necessary part of life can be a big step toward health for Peacemakers. It can wake them up. They need to learn that honest disagreements sometimes need to take place, without needing to smooth them over.

Part of the healing process for Nines is linked to their disconnection from the Pearl Essence – Autonomy. Peacemakers need to acknowledge and honor that their needs to be appreciated and seen. They somehow turned their backs on the Pearl Essence in order to be ordinary and supportive to others. The line between Three and Nine indicates this disconnection from Essence. Nines need to reawaken their desire to be the center of attention, to play a central role in their own life. Too often they take a back seat to others or get stuck in a support role. Too often they lose themselves in harmonizing relations with others. Peacemakers need to start going for themselves, taking the initiative, realizing some of their dreams. This may also mean waking up the Red Essence inside of them, especially its passion and dynamism.

LEADERSHIP AND ORGANIZATIONS

Nine leaders know how to get the best out of the people they work with. They are generally genial and nondirective in their leadership. Nine managers establish warm relationships with people. They don't want to tell others what to do but rather encourage them to move on their own understanding and initiative. This leaves employees plenty of latitude in carrying out directives. They do not pressure employees to get the job done. Nine leaders often avoid decisions or render those decisions in a way that is diffuse or unclear to others. They avoid decisions in diverse ways, such as asking for more information or counseling caution. Often they decide not to decide. The decisions themselves are motivated by the desire to create consensus, to find common ground between competing options.

Though Nines are easygoing and inclusive in their style of management, they can also be stubborn and intransigent. They cannot be pressured in any way, as they will just put you on permanent "hold" if they feel pressured. Nine managers can also be careless about details or negligent in both follow-up and follow-through. One of their principal strategies is to delay action, and it does not always serve their purpose. Their desire to be calm and unflappable can also result in not paying attention to what needs urgent attention. They can easily get sidetracked, missing what is really important.

Nine organizations at their best are reliable, dependable organizations where there is a lot of teamwork, cooperation, communication and harmony. These are not usually organizations that function well in high stress environments or in highly competitive markets. Post offices, insurance companies and big bureaucracies are usually Nine organizations. At their worst, they can be sleepy, slow moving and mired in routine, procedures and seniority. Resignation and passivity remove any chance of individual initiative and the whole organization grinds on with a kind of hopeless inertia. At their best, they are creating order out of chaos, performing reasonably well in a tough situation.

WORKING WITH NINES

Nines generally prefer to work in a team. They are good with cooperation and teamwork. They are sensitive to the full range of opinions in a team. They need to know their place and be part of a well-functioning routine. They sometimes get stuck in procedures that are too strict or irrelevant. Don't expect them to meet deadlines. Be aware of the fact that they may have difficulty prioritizing, determining the importance of different priorities. If you pressure Nines, they will slow down, shut down or become unfocused. Forcing them to be confrontational will have a similar unwanted result. On the other hand, the Nine desire to avoid conflict may prevent them from working through important issues.

There is a need to be diplomatic with Nines, moving incrementally from the familiar to the unfamiliar. You create rapport with Nines by talking slowly, focusing on the positive, being agreeable, dwelling on what is familiar, staying calm, avoiding conflict and seeing the good in others.

COLLECTIVE EXPRESSIONS OF THE PEACEMAKER

India represents the archetypal Nine country. Throughout its history India has absorbed wave after wave of invasions, generally without much resistance. It has remained passive, and that passivity has only been shaken off in recent times. Gandhi's idea of satyagraha or passive resistance is a uniquely Indian idea that is aligned with the Nine fixation – stubbornly resisting but attempting to avoid conflict. The law of karma and the belief in reincarnation has made Indians very passive in their acceptance of the circumstances of their lives, always with the hope of getting a better life the next time around. The caste system and early marriage decreed by parents or village elders have contributed to this passivity. This social rigidity has been coupled with government bureaucracies that have rivaled anything on earth for their inertia, corruption, and the slowness of their responses to human needs. And even if modern India is in the grip of fabulous changes, Indians are still generally passive in their approach to life.

Although Indians never say no, they don't exactly do what you want them to do either. They wag their heads pleasantly, but somehow the job never gets done, or it gets done with long delays, or it gets done in a way that is of little use to anyone. This is the traditional passive-aggressive approach of the Nine, having in it the elements of stubbornness, inertia, being spaced out and cruising in the habitual. Delaying decisions or actions and not being honest about it is one of the primary strategies of Indian businessmen - and it causes tremendous difficulties in their relationships with Western corporations, which generally expect deadlines to be met or to be informed when deadlines cannot be met.

The relationship to anger in India is basically denial. Indians are not aware of their anger. Although there is horrific violence in the culture – violence toward women, toward children, toward the lower castes, sectarian violence and so on – this violence is not seen as a result of anger. Indians don't feel they are angry. And if you get angry with Indians, they just go blank. They shut down. They don't understand and they will make you pay for your anger at a later date. Anger is not okay, conflict is not okay, and the expression of anger threatens the basic order of existence.

Although there is a lot of activity in Indians that fits the Nine fixation perfectly, there is also a lot of the quality of the Living Daylight in the collective. India has a quality of the heart that can only be described as the Living Daylight. Many foreigners sense this quality from the first moment they arrive in India. Despite conditions that are sometimes appalling, this quality of the heart comes through - the basic goodness of existence.

Canada, Austria, the Baltic republics and many of the former states of the Soviet block are Nine countries, as this is often the fixation of countries that are forced to adapt to the demands of stronger neighbors. People are pleasant, accommodating and reticent. They don't easily come out with their own opinions or draw attention to themselves. They have the traditional reserve of the Nine; the tendency not to express themselves unless specifically asked to do so.

CHAPTER 10

MATURITY

The development of an aware ego is a lifework for all of us. It is the basis of real maturity. We need a mature personality in order to live our lives to the full extent of our capacities. Developing an aware ego means that we graduate from the realm of fusion and unhealthy dependency on others. We stop getting lost in the other. We no longer live in the romantic dream or the illusion that one person is going to fulfill all our needs. We become less reactive and compulsive in our behaviors. We are no longer the object of our compulsions, our emotional reactions, our fears and our shame – they no longer disconnect us from our sense of self.

Maturity means we that we become more our own person, standing up for our values and what we think is right. We leave behind the world of unhealthy differentiation, entitlement and power struggles. We are our own person, but we no longer need to compete with others, dominate or control others. We develop a genuine capacity to support others. The development of an aware ego means that we become more aware of our needs, our values, our desires and our limitations. We can express our needs, wants and desires in a healthy way. We move naturally toward what we need and what our heart desires. We take responsibility for our lives and for our actions.

Becoming more mature in our relationships is a sign of the development of an aware ego. Aware ego means that we recognize our uniqueness as well as our similarities with others. We do not move away from others because we are different from them. We have a healthy sense of self that flourishes in the diversity of our relationships. We are comfortable in our aloneness and in being with others. Our couple relationship becomes a place where we grow and do the work on ourselves. We feel solid in the relationship and solid in ourselves.

Aware ego means awareness of our fixation. It means that we are no longer at the mercy of our fixation and that we have more inner space. We begin to spend more time in the experiences of Essence than in experiences of fixation, and we can clearly distinguish between the two. We understand the relationship between Essence and fixation, and how to explore and integrate Essence. We know when we are connected to a particular quality of Essence and when we are disconnected. We can contain the experiences of Essence and the frustration or discomfort that occur when Essence is not available. We know that we have integrated many qualities of Essence and we trust life to bring us the experiences we need to continue to integrate Essence.

An aware ego means we that we develop a mature sense of self that is informed by Being. Facing the issues of our personality helps us to integrate Essence and develop an aware ego. These two processes are happening simultaneously - integrating Essence and developing an aware ego. The Enneagram is a brilliant tool in this work because it not only shows us the precise relationship between ego and Being, it shows us the cognitive mistake of the ego in relation to Being. It points us in the right direction, namely the direction of Essence and Being, while at the same time supporting our individuation, maturity and healthy ego functioning.

When we have enlightenment experiences, as in the experiences of satori or moksha, there is an abrupt discontinuity in our identification with our conditioning, our fixation, our thought patterns, our self-images and beliefs. What we are experiencing is a powerful but temporary "dis-identification" with our ego self. We are not experiencing the dissolution of ego structure, which is apparently responsible for functions as basic as language, thinking and self-preservation. We cannot function without an ego structure. In adults, the lack of ego structure or a weak ego structure indicates pathology and personality disorder, not enlightenment.

The work with Essence and the Enneagram does not dissolve our ego structure or our fixation. The work makes us more aware of our ego structure and our fixation. Integrating Essence facilitates the development of a resilient, stable, freely functioning ego. By integrating Essence we are constructing the wholeness of our personhood. We are constructing a mature selfhood. We become more and more human, more aware of our personal reality.

The Enneagram has been a powerful tool in the transformation of my life and my work with others. It is a synthesis of spiritual and psychological understanding that is still developing rapidly. I have attempted to present this synthesis in simple, direct language. What I have presented here *is* simple, but not easy. Thanks to the development of the modern Enneagram, there is a system wherein psychology and spirituality can actually embrace and illuminate each other, rather than disown each other. Through the work with

Essence and the Enneagram, I have been able to heal many of the conflicts between my spiritual aspirations and my personal psychology. I hope that others may experience a similar healing through this book.

AFTERWORD

I intentionally left out many of the key elements of a traditional Enneagram book. In particular, I omitted any explanation of the wings, the arrows and the subtypes. I felt this material would detract from the primary focus of the book, which is Essence and how it relates to the personality types of the Enneagram. I did not want to load the book down with too much information about the fixations, since there are already many excellent books that contain this information.

SUGGESTED READING

Almaas, A. H., Essence – *The Diamond Approach to Inner Realization*, York Beach, Samuel Weiser, 1986.

Almaas, A. H., *Facets of Unity*, Berkeley, Diamond Books, 1998.

Almaas, A. H., *The Pearl Beyond Price*, Berkeley, Diamond Books, 1988.

Almaas, A. H., *Space Cruiser Inquiry*, Boston, Shambhala Publications, 2002.

Barks, Coleman, *Essential Rumi*, San Francisco, Harper, 1997.

Goldberg, Michael J., *Nine Ways of Working*, New York, Marlowe, 1996.

Gurdjieff, George Ivanovich, *Meetings with Remarkable Men*, New York, Penguin, 1991.

Mahler, Margaret S., *The Psychological Birth of the Human Infant*, Basic Books, 1975.

Maitri, Sandra, *The Spiritual Dimension of the Enneagram*, New York, Penguin Putnam, 2001.

Naranjo, Claudio, *Character and Neurosis*, Nevada City, Gateways, 1994.

Osho, *The Psycholology of the Esoteric*, New York, Harper and Rowe, 1979.

Ouspensky, P. D., *In Search of the Miraculous*, New York, Harcourt, 2005.

Schnarch, David, *Passionate Marriage*, New York, Henry Holt, 1997.

Trungpa, Chogyam, *Cutting Through Spiritual Materialism*, Boulder, Shambhala Publications, 1973.

Trungpa, Chogyam, *Shambhala – The Sacred Path of the Warrior*, Boulder, Shambhala Publications, 1984.

Viorst, Judith, *Necessary Losses*, New York, Simon and Schuster, 1998.

O

is a symbol of the world,
of oneness and unity. O Books
explores the many paths of wholeness
and spiritual understanding which
different traditions have developed down
the ages. It aims to bring this knowledge
in accessible form, to a general readership,
providing practical spirituality to today's seekers.

For the full list of over 200 titles covering:

- CHILDREN'S PRAYER, NOVELTY AND GIFT BOOKS
- CHILDREN'S CHRISTIAN AND SPIRITUALITY
- CHRISTMAS AND EASTER
- RELIGION/PHILOSOPHY
- SCHOOL TITLES
- ANGELS/CHANNELLING
- HEALING/MEDITATION
- SELF-HELP/RELATIONSHIPS
- ASTROLOGY/NUMEROLOGY
- SPIRITUAL ENQUIRY
- CHRISTIANITY, EVANGELICAL AND LIBERAL/RADICAL
- CURRENT AFFAIRS
- HISTORY/BIOGRAPHY
- INSPIRATIONAL/DEVOTIONAL
- WORLD RELIGIONS/INTERFAITH
- BIOGRAPHY AND FICTION
- BIBLE AND REFERENCE
- SCIENCE/PSYCHOLOGY

Please visit our website,
www.O-books.net

Aim for the Stars...Reach the Moon
How to coach your life to spiritual and material success
Conor Patterson
A fascinating, intelligent, and beneficial tool and method of programming your mind for success. The techniques are fast to achieve, motivating, and inspiring. I highly recommend this book.
Uri Geller
1905047274 208pp **£11.99 $19.95**

Amulets
Kim Farnell
This is a wonderful book for those interested in learning about amulets and how to create them. Farnell's expertise makes her the ideal guide. Her knowledge is sound and her instructions are always clear and easy to follow. The strength of this book lies in it being one of easy access and also very well presented in its structure and internal logic. It makes an ideal reference book for anyone of a serious interest, being equally suited to beginners and experts alike.
Deborah Houlding, author of The Houses: Temples of the Sky
1846940060 160pp **£9.99 $14.95**

Developing Spiritual Intelligence
The power of you
Altazar Rossiter
This beautifully clear and fascinating book is an incredibly simple guide to that which so many of us search for: the kind of spiritual

intelligence that will enable us to live peacefully, intelligently, and joyfully whatever our circumstances. It brings the spiritual world down to earth, which is just where we need it to be in order to take our next step. **Dr Dina Glouberman** author of Life Choices, Life Changes and co-founder of Skyros
1905047649 240pp **£12.99 $19.95**

Happiness in 10 Minutes
Brian Mountford
Brian Mountford-in exploring "happiness"-celebrates the paradox of losing and finding at its heart. At once both profound and simple, the book teaches us that to be fully alive is to be in communion and that gratitude leads us into the mystery of giving ourselves away-the path of true joy. **Alan Jones**, Dean of Grace Cathedral, San Francisco, author of Reimagining Christianity.
1905047770 128pp b/w illustrations **£6.99 $9.95**

Head Versus Heart-and our Gut Reactions
The 21st century enneagram
Michael Hampson
A seminal work, whose impact will continue to reverberate through-out the 21st century because of two original contributions. Firstly, Hampson provides a credible, coherent and compelling explanation of the inter relationships between the nine categories of the Enneagram recast as the Strategy Board. Secondly, he has generalised the Enneagram so that it can be used as a tool of analysis in many fields of human endeavour, bringing illumination and allowing insights to tumble out. **Fr Alexander**, Worth Abbey
19038169000 320pp **£11.99 $16.95**